LET'S
FLIP
THE
SCRIPT

African American Life Series

*A complete listing of the books
in this series
can be found at
the back of this volume.*

LET'S
FLIP
THE
SCRIPT

AN AFRICAN AMERICAN DISCOURSE ON LANGUAGE, LITERATURE, AND LEARNING

KEITH GILYARD

WAYNE STATE UNIVERSITY PRESS
DETROIT

99 98 97 96   5 4 3 2 1

Library of Congress Cataloging-in-Publication Data
Gilyard, Keith, 1952–
Let's flip the script : an African American discourse on language,
literature, and learning / Keith Gilyard.
p.   cm. — (African American life series)
Includes bibliographical references and index.
ISBN 0-8143-2645-5 (pbk. : alk. paper)
1. Language and education—United States. 2. Language and languages—Political
aspects. 3. Afro-Americans—Education. 4. American fiction—Afro-American authors
—History and criticism. I. Title. II. Series.
P40.8.G55   1996
407'.073—dc20   96–16292

CONTENTS

——

INTRODUCTION

MUCH TO MY BENEFIT, I have friends and colleagues who encourage me to say things about language and education, particularly with respect to African Americans. They solicit writing, invite me to forums, and prop me up at podiums. They generally seek insight, decisiveness, and controversy, though I wonder sometimes which they most prefer. Notwithstanding, I am thankful for the opportunities to influence discussion and, possibly, to shape actual maneuvers. The eleven essays in this book, each written upon request, indicate the major themes with which I have been concerned during the past five years. They furthermore represent my overall attempt to shift discourses and activities, to turn the tide or flip the script.

The first two essays, "A Heightened Sense of Language" and "The Social Responsibility That Writing Is," deal pointedly with confluences of language and politics. Within the context of considering diversity issues, I demonstrate how language resonates politically and how value-laden writing pedagogy is. Although I admittedly digress a bit, my specific purpose is to spark resistance to counterproductive language arts instruction.

The next three essays comprise a sort of unit on literature and teaching. When my 1980s research in sociolinguistics made me conscious of the frequency with which musings about linguistic strength and weakness constituted motifs in African American literary works, I began to write a series of pieces reflecting this understanding. "Genopsycholinguisticide and the Language Theme in African American Fiction" is the most expansive. "Tucept HighJohn and the Limits of Language Programming" carries the argument and way of reading a step further, and "Julius and Jesse in 003" shows how the critical agenda I pursued can meaningfully inform writing classrooms.

The remaining essays can profitably stand alone. "One More Time for Professor Nuruddin" is a "knowledge loan" to Yusuf Nuruddin, the resident scholar of Bedford-Stuyvesant. I have tried to lay out in concise and accessible fashion the origin, development, and educational implications of Africanized forms of English. It is a pleasure to do so, but Yusuf still has to pay me back.

"Language Learning and Democratic Development" is in many ways a homage to the "NYU crew." In consulting and learning with people affiliated with New York University's Program in English Education, some of whom I'll name later, I was pressed to consider seriously, always with the intent of shaking things up, notions of democracy and their relationship to various educational practices.

"African American in Process" investigates the claim, to which Lisa Delpit's work is central, that writing-process methodology is inappropriate for African American students. I argue, conversely, that process instruction is indeed fitting instruction for such students and that teachers can more fruitfully challenge the abuse of process methods than the process paradigm itself.

"A Legacy of Healing" largely examines the generative power of African American folkloric, literary, and educational traditions with the idea of harnessing some of that power to revamp schooling. In addition, recounting my role in one contentious discussion of education, I aim to illustrate briefly how language theorists can contribute to practical debates.

"Getting Off the Hook" encodes my obligation to respond to *The Bell Curve.* There is hardly need for further prefatory comment on this score. On its own, the essay won't win an intellectual tug of war with the Herrnstein and Murray book, but I know there's plenty of help out there, with more coming.

Writing the closing essay, "Playing with the Patterns," was perhaps the most fun. I have tried to account for the early influences on my present teaching beliefs and style. Such an autobiographical attempt inevitably falls somewhat shy of the mark, but I think it reveals valuable perspectives on (dis)connections between curricular and extracurricular activity.

This book should especially please those who put me up to it. I was not always an eager participant, and I am even tempted to abandon protocol at this point and take sole credit for whatever good parts there may be and blame them for the faults. Most of them would appreciate that bit of mischief, but I'll refrain and give propers in the usual way. All kidding aside, they have my utmost gratitude:

Lillian Bridwell-Bowles, former president of the Conference on College Composition and Communication; Geneva Smitherman, solid sista force throughout; Claire Wood and the members of the City University of New York Writing Centers Association; Kenneth Peeples, editor of *Community Review*; James Raymond, Nancy Johnson, and Reginald Martin, editors of the special African American literature issue of *College English*; Edison O. Jackson, president of Medgar Evers College, CUNY; Frances Degan Horowitz, president of the CUNY Graduate School; Ira Shor and the faculty of CUNY's Ph.D. program in English; Brenda Greene, who pulled me into her NCTE panel on cultural and critical literacy; the students of Medgar Evers College, especially the data producers who have consented to assist; John Garvey of the CUNY Office of Academic Affairs; Rita Brause, Nancy Lester, John Mayher, and Cynthia Onore, that NYU connection; Ruth Vins and Clifford Hill, Teachers College, Columbia University; Yusuf Nuruddin once again, who keeps me on my toes; Clinton Crawford, a positive force as well; Steve Cannon, who forced me into the *Curve*, not to mention many previous ventures; and Richard Larson and Tom McCracken, who sought narrative. I'll even add a tad more.

"Education, education," the youthful man would repeat as his health failed beneath the Georgia sun. "Make sure to educate the boys," he would scribble in the diary to be left for his wife. He in fact had been promised by a friend, a school official, that the friend would see the man's two sons through college. The man also had two daughters, but he had a different vision for them. Quite predictably. It was 1936. But we also know that the twist, the flip, is often the most important part of the tale. One of the man's daughters, nine years old at the time of his death, grew up remembering her father's words. "Education, education," she would stress repeatedly, decades later, to her son, who, most days, is looking for some educational action.

Mad thanks to Charles Otis Lewis and his daughter Mary.

I also want to thank Juanita Horan and George Rhinehart, my colleagues in the Syracuse University Writing Program, for keeping technological breakdowns from becoming nervous ones. And lastly, I wish to acknowledge the contributions of Dr. Teresa M. Redd of Howard University and Dr. Charles Coleman of York College, CUNY. Possessed of brilliant minds and helping spirits, they reviewed the manuscript thoroughly and provided much-needed guidance. "My bad" if it turns out that I have not taken full advantage of their wisdom.

K. G.

LANGUAGE
AND
POLITICS

A Heightened Sense of Language as Educational and Social Critique

I HAVE LONG BEEN SENSITIVE to how certain terminology informs my perception, partly because of my role in a mass search for an adequate name. Having been Colored, Negro, Black (sometimes with a lower-case b), Afro-American, and African American (sometimes with a hyphen) all in only four decades, I have had to examine closely several linguistic constructs just to figure out my cultural identity. Also, on a more personal level, I possessed an early sense of language as a tool to be manipulated beyond the purposes of everyday communication. I can recall writing poems as far back as the third grade. A teacher even noted on my permanent record card, a usually dreadful document maintained by the New York City Board of Education, that poetry writing was a great interest of mine. Of course, we know by now that I found my way into the English profession and into print as a poet, two results that do not often enough follow from childhood language experiences such as I have described. My language interest, inventiveness, and playfulness were kept alive and developed, despite various obstacles, and my book *Voices of the Self: A Study of Language Competence* exists as the most noteworthy extension of those urges. Perhaps some brief retrospection about creating the manuscript is appropriate before I

Presented April 1, 1993, at the Conference on College Composition and Communication at a session linked to a revisiting of *Students' Right to Their Own Language*.

13

comment upon the *Students' Right** resolution and how the doctrine of linguistic equality it champions still sparks arguments. I also intend, in raising the general question of language awareness, to offer my own sociolinguistic takes on the war in the Persian Gulf and the uprising in Los Angeles, as well as to consider a few terms that are not understood well enough by many educators, namely, *whiteness, multiculturalism,* and *dialect interference.*

I arrived at the 1983 convention in Detroit in search of a dissertation topic. Gordon Pradl, the faculty member with whom I worked most closely during my days at New York University, had been encouraging me to conduct research related to Black English Vernacular, as we called it at the time. His suggestion was an outgrowth of discussions about language acquisition in a course he taught. Of particular interest to me was how bidialectal speakers, such as myself, grow to assign values and uses to each dialect, and I began a review of the literature. However, I was not confident about the contribution I could make until I attended a session in Detroit entitled "Black Student Writers and Linguistic Implications for Social Change" and heard Geneva Smitherman cite the need, as a complement to other theoretical work, for self-investigations by those who alternate or code-switch between BEV and Standard English.

I had my project. I dusted off an autobiographical narrative I had shelved several years earlier, decided to make the case academically that it represented a valuable record of bidialectal language development, and planned to pair the story in some way with analyses I would make of selected scholarship pertinent to BEV and education. I consulted works such as Albert E. Stone's *Autobiographical Occasions and Original Acts* and James Olney's *Metaphors of Self,* growing certain in the process that my narrative, though necessarily inaccurate as chronicle, was yet legitimate psychological history. From Elliot Eisner's work, I drew intellectual justification for artistic research, thus ridding myself once and for all of anxiety about validity and the lack of statistical data. In addition, I delved deeper into linguistic and educational literature, coming across as-

*Drafted in 1972, the *Students' Right* resolution was adopted by the Conference on College Composition and Communication in Anaheim in 1974. The resolution affirms "the students' right to their own patterns and varieties of language" and that "teachers must have the experiences and training that will enable them to respect diversity." Later that year, a background statement and a bibliography were included in *College Composition and Communication.*

14

sertions such as R. A. Hudson's, in *Sociolinguistics*, that "one of the most solid achievements of linguistics in the twentieth century has been to eliminate the idea (at least among professional linguists) that some languages or dialects are inherently better than others" (191), and J. L. Dillard's, in *Black English*, that "it's possible to characterize a peach as a deficient apple; in fact, it's the only conclusion you can come to if you judge the peach by the apple's standards" (33). I discovered the remark of Joshua Fishman and Erika Lueders-Salmon in "What Has the Sociology of Language to Say to the Teacher?" that "the home and regional speech can be used for many purposes in school" (78). And, perhaps most important, I happened upon *Students' Right to Their Own Language*, a special issue of *College Composition and Communication*, a document that synthesizes progressive sociolinguistic thought and mightily informs *Voices of the Self*.

There has been a professional dimension, then, to my heightened language sensibility. In my work I have remained true to the spirit of *Students' Right* and stand ever ready to criticize attitudes and policies about linguistic difference that are harmful to students. Recently, for example, while I was mentoring a group of graduate students who were studying the teaching of basic writing, several principles of linguistic diversity became crucial to our discussion. The notion of linguistic competence, that is, the idea that every speaker has unconsciously mastered the language variety of his or her native community, was easy enough for them to accept. But some took exception to my contention that any such language variety mastered was equal to any other in terms of ability to express concepts. We had a spirited debate. Students made arguments that certain Asians would be unable to say "I want to be left alone," because individualism is not a desirable cultural trait for them, that some languages lack a highly technological or scientific vocabulary, even that Joseph Conrad's choice to write in English must have had something to do with the superiority of the language. My rebuttals, however, flowed easily. Assuming that a yearning for solitude is odd in an Asian culture (and none of my Asian friends and colleagues have assured me that this is categorically the case), it is still not an impossible idea to hold individually or to express linguistically. I could argue for African American political superiority in the United States, a rather remote possibility but not at all difficult to put into words. I can easily enough *say* that Black folk should control all the money, munitions, media, and legislatures. As for terminology, any language can add it, just as *AIDS* has shown up in recent dictionaries. And Conrad's choice had exclusively to do with his feelings toward English, not any particular merits of English itself. Similarly, his choice to be known as Joseph Conrad instead of Jozef Korzeniowski (first and last names) or Jozef Konrad (first and one of several middle names) had nothing to do with the superiority of English names or English spelling, not to mention that one of Conrad's contemporaries, Henryk Sienkiewicz—a Pole writing in Polish—won the Nobel Prize for Literature.

Although our debate centered on comparisons among languages, I stressed that the concept of linguistic equality holds true for dialects of any given language as well. Chauvinism about foreign languages and chauvinism about dialects, an idea more relevant for most writing teachers, are but two sides of the same coin.

An expressly sociolinguistic viewpoint continues to help shape my larger social outlook as well. In fact, it's impossible to distinguish at times between my macro-level social concerns and strictly educational ones because all my language insights eventually find expression in my classrooms and lead to increased awareness about both writing and language in general. A few more examples will underscore this point.

The Persian Gulf War brought us a baffling array of terms such as *aerial sorties* and *collateral damage*, words aimed to distance combat from carnage in the minds of the American public and make the conflict palatable. There have been voluminous remarks in this vein. But I submit, too, that certain justificative language was directed specifically at the African American community by Secretary of State James Baker, who, upon returning from a tense negotiating session with Iraqi representative Tariq Assiz, declared that Assiz had "dissed" him. I had never known Baker to be an aficionado of the African American vernacular—never *could* know from all the Standard English he spoke in public. Is it far-fetched, therefore, to suggest that his use of *dissed* was an effort to pitch the war to the African American community, one overrepresented in the military, in phrasing it could understand and support? Certainly many Black folk, for better or worse, accept the premise that harsh retaliation must follow being "dissed." We witnessed a major demonstration of such thinking after the verdict in the Rodney King case, another situation (w)rapped in language that should be scrutinized. The idea of revolt or organized violence was played down in media reportage, where the explosive aftermath of the verdict was generally characterized as a "riot," a relatively thoughtless outburst.

How you respond to these messages has to do with your political sense, of course. I have no particular interest in that at this point. But even to recognize the issues I am raising reflects the heightened language sensibility I am concerned with as a citizen and educator. Reportage of the war and the King case became subject matter in my courses, a practice in line with the sentiment expressed by participants at the 1987 English Coalition Conference, who wrote in the conference report that one of their goals was to have students "recognize and evaluate the ways in which others use language to affect them" (Lloyd-Jones and Lunsford 19).

Another interesting item for students and teachers to consider is one current proposal for countering social ills: the abolition of the white race—linguistically. This is the position taken by the editors of the journal *Race Traitor*, who view "whiteness" as a construct of privilege and not as a biological or racial descriptor (something it can only be inadequately). As they explain:

> Our primary intended audience consists of those people commonly called "whites" who sense whiteness to be a problem for themselves and others. For these people, "race treason," in our view, best sums up the meaning of consistent opposition to white supremacy. We hope that Afro-Americans [they're a few beats behind with that term] and other people of color will see this project as consistent with their own efforts, and we hope it will stimulate discussion among all opponents of white power. We appreciate the unique contributions that persons of color, who have a wealth of experience with white authority, can make to undermining it, and we invite all interested persons to write for *Race Traitor* and make whatever use of it they can (Garvey et al. 126–27).

"Race treason" imbues public discourse with freshness, a quality also needed in educational debates. Theorists like John Mayher are keenly aware of this imperative. His trademark word, *uncommonsense*, moves discussion forward in ways that *progressive* and *conservative* do not—at least not any longer. Mayher knows that the theories we hold implicitly are the ones that generally guide us most powerfully. We will not change what we never bother to call into question. Uncommonsense, then, is a strong empirical questioning of common sense ideas and a commitment to examine our received wisdom at the conscious level. It insists upon change, not boisterously, but nonetheless. We can unearth, rather dispassionately, the authoritarian and behaviorist underpinnings of transmission-style instruction. Only through such activity can we meaningfully adopt the developmental and constructionist perspectives we are urged, sometimes in shrill tones, to embrace.

Not all new language, however, serves to clarify. *Multiculturalism* is a case in point. Flawed as an educational concept at the outset, it is now hopelessly clichéd and does what all clichés do: name complex phenomena vaguely. It is best used to describe a population, not an educational program, for any coherent program has to take up deeper questions. How, for example, do we avoid trivializing the struggles of certain groups whose confronting of racism and exclusion led, as was proper, to the rhetoric of multiculturalism in the first place? The more "multi" multiculturalism gets, the more it deflects attention from the cultural contributions of any one ethnic group. So a successful African American challenge, say, to exclusion may subsequently lead, in many current multicultural programs, to virtual re-exclusion. This is not to argue that wide representation is uncalled for; I am merely suggesting that the matter is quite complicated and not resolvable through hackneyed expressions. I have been offering the term *transculturalism* as a better description of certain educational initiatives that emphasize specific transactions among students from various cultural and ethnic backgrounds as opposed to being primarily concerned with "exposure."

I will call attention to one more coinage, *dialect interference.* Although not a new term, I hear it frequently and confusedly associated with writing instruction or, more precisely, writing problems. As such, it requires renewed inspection.

It is a simple matter to demonstrate how any variety of English *may* interfere with the production of an alternative variety. I jotted down the following conversation I had with a student from Jamaica as I was entering the building where I work. She owed me an assignment:

(1) You get my paper, professor?
(2) No, where did you leave it?
(3) I leave it in your mailbox.
(4) When?
(5) I leave it in your mailbox yesterday.

Sentences 3 and 5 represent a Jamaican language variety that features a largely uninflected verb system that marks time by context and helping words such as *yesterday. I leave* in each instance

18

represents what we would commonly call first-person past tense. If this student's intention were to write in Standard English and she produced these types of sentences in her texts, dialect interference would be cited by many, somewhat correctly, as the reason. I would add, however, that a nonstandard dialect can only be a writing problem to the extent that the writer relies solely upon native oral resources to meet the demands of writing Standard English. If, to the contrary, strong reading ears and writing voices have been developed relative to Standard English, those tools, not the nonstandard dialect, would dominate writing situations where producing Standard English is the writer's goal. In other words, nonstandard dialect cannot function in isolation as a writing problem. The student who employed in her speech the verb system demonstrated above used no such constructions in any of her papers, most of which were written in class. No dialect correction program is necessary in her case or in the case of any other writer. Time is best spent fostering the differentiation that generally must occur between speech and writing personae.

A librarian in Brooklyn invited me to her institution to make a presentation about African American literature. During the session, I read from several of Charles Chesnutt's Uncle Julius stories, which are written partly in African American Vernacular English. During the ensuing exchange, an African American woman asked me bluntly, "What do you think about Black English?" Before I could answer, she declared, "I hate it." I could not persuade her to feel otherwise (or, at least, she wouldn't admit it), though our dialogue was very time-consuming. In fact, I didn't get to discuss with the audience Chesnutt's considerable literary skill.

In a university workshop, several writing instructors told me quite forcefully that part of their responsibility is to correct the speech of students, an activity that, even if they could do it, which is highly doubtful, contributes nothing, as I hope to have illustrated, to sensible writing instruction. Fortunately, not all their colleagues agreed with them.

These exchanges happened much closer to the millennium than to 1974, when *Students' Right* appeared. A major mission for us is to continue, the best we can, to disturb the intellectual comfort zones of those whose views of language variety would penalize rather than aid students. Our understanding of language and our language itself must be superior if we are to reflect our discipline at its most accomplished level and help move educational programs forward productively.

WORKS CITED

Corbett, Edward P. J., ed. *Students' Right to Their Own Language.* Special issue of *College Composition and Communication* 25 (Fall 1974).

Dillard, J. L. *Black English: Its History and Usage in the United States.* New York: Vintage, 1973.

Eisner, Elliot. "On the Difference between Scientific and Artistic Approaches to Qualitative Research." *Educational Researcher* (April 1981): 5–9.

Fishman, Joshua A., and Erika Lueders-Salmon. "What Has the Sociology of Language to Say to the Teacher? On Teaching the Standard Variety to Speakers of Dialectal or Sociolectal Varieties." In *Functions of Language in the Classroom*, ed. C. B. Cazden et al. New York: Teachers College Press, 1972. 67–83.

Garvey, John, et al. "Correspondence." *Race Traitor* (Winter 1993): 126–27.

Gilyard, Keith. *Voices of the Self: A Study of Language Competence.* Detroit: Wayne State UP, 1991.

Hudson, R. A. *Sociolinguistics.* Cambridge: Cambridge UP, 1980.

Lloyd-Jones, Richard, and Andrea A. Lunsford, eds. *The English Coalition Conference: Democracy through Language.* Urbana, IL: NCTE/MLA, 1989.

Mayher, John S. *Uncommon Sense: Theoretical Practice in Language Education.* Portsmouth, NH: Boynton/Cook, 1990.

Olney, James. *Metaphors of Self: The Meaning of Autobiography.* Princeton, NJ: Princeton UP, 1972.

Stone, Albert E. *Autobiographical Occasions and Original Acts: Versions of American Identity from Henry Adams to Nate Shaw.* Philadelphia: U of Pennsylvania P, 1982.

THE SOCIAL RESPONSIBILITY
THAT WRITING IS—
AND WRITING INSTRUCTION TOO

WRITING IS NOT AN ACTIVITY that features social responsibility as an option. Writing *is* social responsibility. When you write, you are being responsible to some social entity even if that entity is yourself. You can be irresponsible as a writer, but you cannot be non-responsible.

This issue probably has been discussed most in literary circles, couched in the long-running debate between those who view art as propaganda and those who subscribe to the notion of art for art's sake. I am obviously in the former camp and feel, for example, that the late critic Addison Gayle spoke compellingly when he asserted at the National Black Writers Conference in 1986 that "if Black people are being shipped to die in Grenada and you choose to write poems and novels about sunsets and trees, you are being responsible. You are just being responsible to the status quo."

At the same gathering, the poet Jayne Cortez reasoned:

> If information is a resource for advancement and development and is the basis by which people make their decisions, then one of the responsibilities of the poet to the community is to provide information. I don't mean merely news reports, statistics, advertisements, or the kind of information some leaders use to assault and manipulate

Presented February 6, 1993, at the Conference of CUNY Writing Centers Association. The conference theme was "Writing and Social Responsibility." Later published in *Community Review* 13.

21

the public, but information detailing significant experiences that would allow a person to use her or his imagination, intelligence, and emotions to gain a greater awareness and understanding of self and the outside world.

Inauguration poetry is certainly intended to be socially responsible writing, whether it is Maya Angelou's official inaugural poem, "On the Pulse of Morning," which seems to fit the Cortez prescription, given Angelou's heartfelt vision of who we are and ought to become as a nation, or Allen Ginsberg's "New Democracy Wish List," the entry, published the same day, that Ginsberg would have read at the ceremony had he been invited. I offer a brief extract:

> Purge U.S. military death squad subsidies in Salvador, Guatemala, etc. We backed up dictators in Zaire, Somalia, Liberia, Sudan, Angola, Haiti, Iran, Iraq, Salvador, we're responsible: admit it then figure ways out. Encourage international trade in Eco-technology in place of enabling codependency on weapons trade. Open CIA & FBI & NSA archives on Cointelpro raids, Government drug dealing, Kennedy/King assassinations, Iranian Contragate, Panama Deception, Vatican, Hand & Lavoro Bank thuggery, etc. including Bush-Noriega relations and other CIA client-agent scandals. (78)

Ginsberg harbors no illusions about art for art's sake. While some readers surely will want to discuss the quality of form, Ginsberg as poet is clearly more interested in the quality of the presidency and other political matters.

Other viewpoints on writing and responsibility, ones more directly related to our work in composition, are revealed in the academic discourse on literacy. Several are touched upon by James Paul Gee in his review of Harvey Graff's *The Legacies of Literacy: Continuities and Contradictions in Western Culture and Society.* Gee first takes up Graff's idea of the literacy myth, that is, the popular notion that literacy is not only requisite for higher-order consciousness but ensures critical thinking, governmental complexity, economic development, and social equity. Concerning the strictly cognitive claims supporting the literacy myth, Gee points to the work of Sylvia Scribner and Michael Cole, *The Psychology of Literacy,* which demonstrates that literacy is not a key variable in the development of ability to reason abstractly. Context proves more salient than the mere fact of literacy.

Graff himself provides ample historical evidence to debunk the social constructs underpinning the literacy myth. For example, the fact that Sweden was the first Western nation to achieve near-universal literacy did not lead to tremendous economic development or social progress. However, one need not scour historical texts very much on this point. Most of us would agree—we know Ginsberg would—that overall development hasn't been ideal in the latter-day United States, where, although the rate of illiteracy is alarming to many, a lot of our most important bad decisions are made by literate people. Even where major social gains have taken place, and the United States fits in here as well, the causes are quite complex. Literacy cannot be extracted from the social matrix and highlighted as the determining factor. In fact, it has been argued that because it privileges certain language interaction, school-based literacy is not a means of ameliorating social inequity but a tool for reproducing it, serving mainly the purposes of the elite. Their particular brands of speech and writing are celebrated; other types are undervalued, discouraged, and penalized. Students generating the latter patterns realize early on, sometimes quite clearly, that the linguistic playing field is tilted against them. Some relish the uphill climb. Many don't even bother, thus falling victim to school systems that purportedly serve their best interests.

The argument being traced here is not that formal literacy instruction has no merit. We should not cease writing and resign our jobs. It is one thing to recognize that some claims about literacy and cognition have been exaggerated, but one need never to have considered literacy and orality a hierarchal proposition, much less one of either/or. Americans of African descent, for example, spring from a tremendous oral tradition but know full well the power of literacy, know it to be strong medicine if for no other reason than the fact that it was in large measure legislated away from them. We're not ambivalent about needing to master both the spoken and the written word. We need to be empowered in as many ways as we can. I would not want to choose between dialogue and writing, between oral tradition and text, between the Negro spirituals that clearly form the basis for Angelou's poem and that poem itself, between this paper I am presenting and the oral exchange I hope will ensue. Literacy has no monopoly on profundity but unmistakably contributes to it—as I am sure any academic who feels he or she has written a brilliant and insightful critique of literacy would agree. Scholars and others are right to warn against abuses of literacy and to rage against language practices that are exclusionary and exploitative. This has been a focus of my own professional endeavors. But any written argument against literacy, including any academic argument against academic literacy, is ultimately, as a philosopher-colleague of mine would say, self-refuting. It reminds me of the paper I heard arguing against the further spread of the English language being delivered, in English, at a conference of English teachers.

This is not a criticism of Gee. He has not taken the position, either in the review essay or in his own book, *Social Linguistics and Literacies*, that literacy is irrelevant. Far from being "anti-literacy," his goals are to force a more careful examination of issues surrounding literacy instruction based upon the understanding that such instruction per se guarantees no particular form of social activity or organization and to keep open the question of how literacy instruction can best contribute to the public good. Gee is as aware as anyone—argues explicitly, in fact—that there never is a neutral literacy agenda. Just as there is no nonresponsible writing, there is no nonresponsible writing instruction. In every act of teaching there is complicity. Or, as he phrases it:

> A text, whether written on paper, on the soul (Plato), or on the world (Freire), is a loaded weapon. The person, the educator, who hands over the gun, hands over the bullets (the perspective), and must own up to the consequences. There is no way out of having an opinion, an ideology, and a strong one. . . . Literacy education is not for the timid. ("The Legacies of Literacy" 208)

What Gee fails to point out, but conceivably could have, is that revolts do occur. Perspectives fall into disfavor. Rulers are toppled. Slaves do forge freedom papers. Personal radicalization can, like Richard Wright's, begin in libraries. In other words, the process of initially becoming literate does not overdetermine how we continue to proceed in our "literateness" since, potentially at least, we are always becoming. Reading, writing, and instruction do act powerfully upon us; at the same time, we can act powerfully on and through reading, writing, and instruction. This is the heart of the matter. The urgent query is not whether we can or cannot write or teach devoid of social responsibility, but whether we dare specify a role for ourselves in situating students in the strongest possible positions relative to our teaching (which means, of course, that in a

24

sense they can overthrow us). Do we deliberately encourage students to be agents of social change? How often, in fact, is the idea that students should change things spelled out in curricula? And I don't mean anything really controversial at this point. (My thing is to restructure society so that material profit for the few is not more important than mass human need, but I know I can't sell this to everybody.) I am merely suggesting that social change is always necessary because, at the very least, what exists is not perfect. But even this mild form of agitation is not championed enough in schools.

In *Writing and Sense of Self*, Robert Brooke distinguishes between the roles of writing students and the roles of writers. In the student role, one habitually follows the dictates of the instructor, learning the strategies and values—both stated and implied—that are issued forth. However, Brooke finds this arrangement unsuitable, possibly debilitating, because it is an attempt to teach writing that has little in common with what motivates practicing writers or how they produce work. He argues, instead:

> Learning to write meaningfully in our culture requires developing an understanding of the self as writer, as someone who uses writing to further personal thinking and to help solve public problems. The development of such a role, such a self-understanding, is more important than developing any set of procedural competencies. Developing such a role, however, depends crucially on connecting the role of self as writer with other roles in the culture outside the classroom, especially writers' roles in the culture at large—including roles for the self as reflective thinker and community influencer. (5)

To Brooke, writers' roles—along with writing itself—are best promoted in a workshop setting steeped in writing-process methodology (multiple drafts, collaboration, alternative purposes and audiences, deferred emphasis on correctness, etc.), and over the years he has shifted his courses in that direction and away from a sequential curriculum emphasizing rhetorical principles. However, because they function within a university, none of Brooke's workshop members fully escape the student role. But in Brooke's view they are able to minimize and/or benefit from the tension involved in negotiating identities relative to both student and writer roles. Joy Ritchie, a participant-observer in a class taught by Brooke, writes that "the workshop classroom values personal experience and self-reflection, tolerance and consideration for plural perspectives, dialogue, responsibility, and commitment to action" (Brooke 139).

Brooke's workshop is admirable, undoubtedly in line with a significant strand of thought in the profession, and is an approach I generally endorse. There is, though, a disturbing aspect. For all their talk about "influencers" and "commitment to action," Brooke and Ritchie avoid indicating what deeds they find commendable. They forward a vague notion of democratic participation as a desirable outcome for their student writers or writer students. Beyond that, they adopt a politically neutral posture, which by now we understand is not an apolitical stance at all, merely one that reflects an unwillingness to articulate political persuasion. To simply advocate social responsibility, once we understand all professional educational activity to be socially responsible, is to advocate nothing. I have asserted the same nothingness many times—quite recently, for that matter—so I am not ridiculing anyone else for doing the same. But I now feel that teachers, including myself, should embrace the honesty that comes with delineating their political views. The point is to truly model mature literacy, to show that literacy always means something in particular. Recalling Gayle, we may pose a question: to whom are you being responsible? Gee causes us to question which type of ammunition is being used. Or, as Richard Bullock, John Trimbur, and Charles Schuster, editors of *The Politics of Writing: Postsecondary*, explain, "we prefer a disciplinary perspective that makes its politics explicit so that all involved— from students and instructors to administrators and theorists—can make intelligent, knowledgeable, informed choices about their own actions" (xviii).

Trimbur closes his own essay in the volume, "Literacy and the Discourse of Crisis" (the literacy crisis is an intellectual kin of the literacy myth), by maintaining that "To counter the growing privatization of education, we need to revive the movement of the late 1960s and early 1970s to democratize higher education through open admissions to *all* colleges and universities, free tuition, and a liveable student stipend" (294).

I don't think this referendum will fly. I think public institutions should remain or become tuition-free, open-admissions entities. I will continue to argue this even though the fight possibly will be lost. I won't, on the other hand, invest much energy debating the stipend issue or the status of private colleges because, though Trimbur's ideas appeal to me, I don't think there is the remotest possibility that fundamental changes will be made in those areas, at least not preceding greater equity and access to quality education in public schools. Although, like Trimbur, I range so far left that I wouldn't register a blip on the radar of what passes for fashionable political conversation in our country these days, there are some struggles I am actually trying to win. But the most important point regarding Trimbur's writing and my pondering it is that his writing about education is expressly political, as must be any response. Writing and writing instruction are socially, not naturally, occurring phenomena. They are never heading nowhere.

WORKS CITED

Brooke, Robert E. *Writing and Sense of Self: Identity Negotiation in Writing Workshops.* Urbana, IL: NCTE, 1991.

Bullock, Richard, John Trimbur, and Charles Schuster, eds. Preface. *The Politics of Writing: Postsecondary.* Portsmouth, NH: Boynton/Cook, 1991. xvii–xx.

Cortez, Jayne. Speech at First National Black Writers Conference at Medgar Evers College, CUNY, March 22, 1986.

Gayle, Addison. Speech at First National Black Writers Conference at Medgar Evers College, CUNY, March 22, 1986.

Gee, James Paul. *Social Linguistics and Literacies: Ideology in Discourses.* New York: Falmer Press, 1990.

———. "The Legacies of Literacy: From Plato to Freire through Harvey Graff." *Harvard Educational Review* 58, No. 2 (1988): 195–212.

Ginsberg, Allen. "New Democracy Wish List." *Newsday,* January 20, 1993. 44, 78.

Graff, Harvey G. *The Legacies of Literacy: Continuities and Contradictions in Western Culture and Society.* Bloomington: Indiana UP, 1987.

Scribner, Sylvia, and Michael Cole. *The Psychology of Literacy.* Cambridge, MA.: Harvard UP, 1981.

Trimbur, John. "Literacy and the Discourse of Crisis." In Richard Bullock et al., eds., *The Politics of Writing Instruction: Postsecondary.* Portsmouth, NH: Boynton/Cook, 1991. 277–95.

LANGUAGE
AND
LITERATURE

GENOPSYCHOLINGUISTICIDE
AND THE LANGUAGE THEME
IN AFRICAN AMERICAN FICTION

> You are a victim of . . . of, let's see, we need a new
> word for it . . . How about: genopsycholinguisticide.
> Sure, why not: "first there was the word . . . and the
> word was nigger," and you became—nigger. And
> that, dear nigger, dear lost, blown-up bleeding,
> stumbling, raggedy nigger, that is genopsycholin-
> guisticide.
>
> Arnold Kemp, Eat of Me: I Am the Savior

THESE SHARP WORDS EMANATING from Yaqui Laster's subconscious
create a key thematic link between *Savior* and numerous other fic-
tions in the African American tradition. In conceiving of genocide
from a psycholinguistic perspective, Kemp has reflected a characteristic language sensibility, an awareness of the linguistics of sub-
jugation. Virtually endless examples abound to reveal the
fascination of African American writers with the Word, with the
idea of language as a force either to prevent or foster the development of authentic selves. As Henry Louis Gates, Jr., has observed,
"the concern to depict the quest of the black speaking subject to
find his or her voice has been a repeated topos of the black tradition, and perhaps has been its most central trope" (*Signifying Monkey* 239).

Language as subject matter is not restricted to Black writing.
Much of Herman Melville's and Mark Twain's work, for example,

Published in *College English* 52, No. 7.

stands as evidence in "mainstream" American literature. Frederick Busch views the dead letter as a central metaphor of Melville's life and work. He explores this idea, in part, by alluding to *Pierre*, the story of a woman who waits seventeen years in vain for a letter from her husband, by noting the report that Bartleby had been a clerk in the Dead Letter Office in Washington, and by citing Billy Budd's stuttering and subsequent silence (analogous to mail not getting through). And in *The Adventures of Tom Sawyer* and *The Adventures of Huckleberry Finn*, Tom's authority over his friends derives from his book knowledge. Pap Finn, on the other hand, forbids Huck to pursue literacy. But in the African American canon, commentary about language is much more common, almost required, and often of a different nature. Any casual critic of the work nods knowingly when Jesse Robinson, the central character in Chester Himes's *The Primitive*, frustrated with racism in general and the racialized politics of corporate publishing in particular, stabs his manuscript with a knife, a scene foreshadowing (quite predictably) the murder of Kriss Cummings.

Houston Baker has traced a language motif in Zora Neale Hurston's *Their Eyes Were Watching God*, as has Barbara Johnson. Mary Helen Washington has contributed a metalinguistic analysis of Gwendolyn Brooks's *Maud Martha*, and Kimberly Benston has advanced a theory, "the topos of (un)naming," that addresses the question of characters choosing or casting off labels as an affirmation of freedom. Language motifs are especially evident in the work of Toni Morrison. Much of *Song of Solomon*, for example, can be viewed in terms of two voyages: the protagonist's journey from Milkman to Macon Dead III to the great-grandson of Shalimar, the flying African, and the movement in the song from Sugarman to Solomon to Shalimar. So, if authors have laid out this specific expressive pattern as one of the distinguishing features of African American literature and laid it out across boundaries of ideology and style, and if eminently qualified critics have responded to it, then what do I propose to add to the mix? The answer is twofold.

First, I am not satisfied with or clear about (which could mean the same thing) explanations offered for why this pattern has manifested itself or, for that matter, about what, outside the author's ethnicity, makes texts "Black." There are those who bristle at the suggestion of racially determined differences in, say, American literature and bristle justifiably (as mongrelized as America is) if a viable cultural-historical explanation of such phenomena is not provided and certain possibilities of texts are ignored. Andrew Delbanco is right, to a degree, when he indicates that a problem in current African American literary criticism is that Black critics tend to exalt what they wish to explain, relying overmuch on a vague concept of Blackness. However, though I think theorists do tend to overstate cases in their zeal to organize canons and/or achieve professional legitimacy, in this matter it is relatively easy to establish an underpinning that supports one distinctive Black quality of the African American literary corpus viewed as a whole.

Consider the oft-debated notion of African survivals, in this instance the conception that cultural practices in Africa can account for certain forms that literature by African Americans has taken. A concise treatment of this idea can be found in Geneva Smitherman's *Talkin and Testifyin*:

> The preslavery background was one in which the concept of Nommo, the magic power of the word, was believed necessary to actualize life and give man mastery over things. All activities of men, and all movements in nature, rest on the word, on the productive power of the word, which is water and heat and seed and Nommo, that is, life force itself. . . . In traditional African culture, a newborn is a mere thing until his father gives and speaks his name. No medicine, potion, or magic of any sort is considered effective without accompanying words. So strong is the African belief in the power and absolute necessity of Nommo that all craftsmanship must be accompanied by speech. (78)

This concept, the argument goes, forms part of a rather fixed African worldview, fuels the much-discussed African oral tradition, and eventually infuses African American written forms with such qualities as testifyin—"a ritualized form of black communication in which the speaker gives verbal witness to the efficacy, truth, and power of some experience in which all blacks have shared" (Smitherman 58)—and signifyin—"the act of talking negatively about somebody through stunning and clever put downs" (82).

The idea of continuity with a generalized African past is provocative but could hardly support a theory by itself, given the shattering transitions surrounding slavery along with a variety of cultural exchanges. But just as features of African languages themselves have survived in creolized forms of English, one would have to assume that African perceptions of language have also become part of the African American cultural matrix. There certainly is enough testifyin and signifyin going on in the literature. Add to this the reality of plantation linguistics, that is, the vocabulary of suppression, the denial of literacy, the devoicing and identity-eradicating imperatives of masters and overseers.

It is obvious, then, why textual comments about language are integral to the African American tradition and why numerous musings about voice imbue the writing of slaves, ex-slaves, and the descendants of slaves. As Gates writes in *Figures in Black: Words, Signs, and the Racial Self*:

> The command of a written language, then, could be no mean thing in the life of the slave. Learning to read, the slave narrative would repeat again and again, was a decisive political act: learning to write, as measured against an eighteenth-century scale of culture and society, was an irreversible step away from the cotton field toward a freedom larger even than physical manumission. (4)

All this is not to delimit explications. African American authors are not solely influenced by African American culture. And, as I mentioned earlier, they aren't the only ones to use language as theme. But, for historical reasons, they do it overwhelmingly, almost inescapably, which is the point.

Among Americans, African Americans know the most about genopsycholinguisticide. Why wouldn't these writers, some of whom are still only four or five generations removed from slavery and living in a society where African Americans to a large degree are still devoiced, take time out to testify? They know they are fortunate to be able to do so. And why not signify? In one sense, they are all taunting lions from trees.

My second purpose in this essay, because I feel theory and practice should remain consciously connected, is to illustrate briefly an interrelationship among African American texts along strict language-as-theme lines. Although, as I pointed out, there is no shortage of critics attentive to sociolinguistic aspects of Black prose, their comments have generally been offshoots of other critical endeavors.

The novels of Alice Walker and Ishmael Reed illustrate my specific concerns. These two writers often have been on opposite sides of the literary fence, so to speak, and, therefore, the choice is a good one to demonstrate that various ideologies often function in African American literature primarily as subsets of an overall preoccupation with the interplay of language and liberation.

II

In *Meridian*, Alice Walker relates the tale of the slave and master storyteller, Louvinie, who has her tongue cut out by her master because she tells a tale of horror so vividly it gives the master's son a fatal heart attack. Mutely, Louvinie begs Master Saxon for the tongue, believing she will be cursed if her tongue, having been removed, is not at least put in a resting place she can designate. If she fails to have this control over her tongue, then the singer in her soul will be doomed, according to the folklore of her native land, "to grunt and snort through eternity like a pig" (44). Louvinie retrieves her tongue from the dirt and buries it under a magnolia tree, a tree that outgrows all others. Other slaves deem the tree magical. They hold that, among other things, it can talk and obscure vision so that slaves in its branches remain undetected.

During a 1960s riot at Saxon College, built on the site of the old Saxon plantation, Louvinie's tree, known as The Sojourner, is destroyed by students. This is the only significant damage they inflict, even though Meridian, one of the students, urges them to wreck the president's house instead. Such disregard or disrespect for their own myth indicates an inability on the part of the so-called radicals to choose effective courses of action. In destroying the fruit of Louvinie's tongue, they forgo mastery of their own.

Walker indeed fingers a problem of the 1960s. One of the difficulties then was judging the sincerity of those who spouted the popular slogans. Without question, there were legions of the committed, but the various shallow ones weren't so easy to distinguish. If the singers in their souls hadn't been lost, those singers couldn't always be trusted. Meridian, who tries to save The Sojourner, is genuine. Metaphorically, she becomes that tree, dedicated to positive advocacy. During a voter registration drive, she tells a man, "You have to get used to using your voice, you know. You start on simple things and move on" (205).

Of course, Louvinie's tongue is not Walker's only tie to an African American fictive tradition. Like Morrison, she's always ready for a naming ritual. In *The Third Life of Grange Copeland*, the naming process defines both a character and society's direct effect upon him. After the Copelands have a child, the father, during his negative "first life," turns despairingly to his equally depressed wife and asks what the boy's name is going to be. She, in turn, names him Brownfield after the brownish, autumnal Georgia cotton fields

35

that blanket their entire world. "That'll do as well as King Albert," the new mother laments. "It won't make a bit of difference what we name him" (178).

The Copelands are the pessimistic or realistic counterparts to the mammy in Charles W. Chesnutt's "A Deep Sleeper," who wants to name her babies Caesar or George Washington. The Copelands don't even dare to hope. Brownfield, then, doesn't start out with much of a chance. It is an explanation of character we don't get concerning Brownfield's literary twin, Mr. _____ of Walker's *The Color Purple*.

Brownfield, like Mr. _____, abuses his wife. Quite naturally, he has to conquer her voice in the process:

> The tender woman he married he set out to destroy. And before he destroyed her he was determined to change her. He was her Pygmalion in reverse. The first thing he started on was her speech. They had begun their marriage with her correcting him, but after a short while this began to wear on him. He could not stand to be belittled at home after coming home from a job that required him to respond to all orders from a stooped position. When she kindly replaced an "is" for an "are" he threw her correction in her face.
>
> "Why don't you talk like the rest of us poor niggers?" he said to her. "Why do you have to be so damn proper? Whether I says 'is' or 'ain't' ain't no damn humping off your butt." (56)

We could side with Brownfield, recalling Celie's comment that "only a fool would want you to talk in a way that feel peculiar to your mind" (*The Color Purple* 194), except that we must recall that Brownfield was initially attracted to Mem because of her knowledge and her educated voice. She had taught him the alphabet and to write his name. He is the one reneging on the deal, relentless in his efforts to make her talk like what she was, "a hopeless nigger woman who got her ass beat every Saturday night" (56). Brownfield eventually murders his wife, an unfortunate woman trapped in the wrong novel. She could have used a Meridian, Shug Avery, that songstress as deliverer, or even Shug's prototype, Hurston's Tea Cake.

In Walker's *The Temple of My Familiar*, the machinations involving language are once more indispensable as the action unfolds. Early in the novel, Carlotta wonders how she and her mother, Zedé, had been able to escape from South America. She thinks that maybe one of the guards was her father and had been perhaps fascinated by the fact that Zedé was literate. Literacy directly associated with the literate subject's freedom is, as we know, common fare. However, Walker inserts a twist. Zedé's literacy frees, instead, Mary Ann Haverstock, a student-victim in La Escuela de Jungla, where Zedé had come to work as a maid-slave. Zedé's fondness for Mary Ann prompts her to write the letter notifying Mary Ann's parents of their daughter's plight, but she is also inspired to "rebel against the gringos and assert who I was. That I could read and write. That I knew reading and writing to have great power" (80). After being taken home by her parents, Mary Ann eventually returns to liberate Zedé and Carlotta and escort them to California, where Carlotta grows up to assume, among others, the role of "guerrilla literaturist."

Another set of characters in *The Temple of My Familiar* achieve knowledge through literacy. Suwelo begins to know his uncle Rafe and become curious about Lissie through the scribbling Rafe left behind on books, notepads, boxes, and napkins. Later, however, Suwelo's failure to read the books that excite Fanny results in their estrangement. Then there is the voice of Lissie Lyles:

> I have always been a black woman. I say that without, I hope, any arrogance or undue pride, for I know this was just luck. I speak of it as luck because of the struggle others have trying to discover who they are and what they should be doing and finding it difficult to know because of all the different and differing voices they are required to listen to. (53)

We find later that Lissie has been insincere: she has experienced incarnations as someone other than a black woman and has indeed suffered the strain of competing voices. Coming to grips with all of them is her essential struggle. Rounding out the novel's obsession with language are Arveyda, a songster; M'Sukta, the African maiden who is held captive in the British Museum of Natural History for fifteen years and who asserts that the words of her native language, inscribed in a mud wall in the simulated village exhibit, were all that kept her going; and Ola, the revolutionary African playwright.

In this novel, which reads to a large degree like a series of seminars, interwoven with the tale are the anticipated linguistics lessons. Ola, for example, addresses the very necessity and origins of language:

> Talk . . . is the key to liberation, one's tongue the very machete of freedom. We are the only species, some say, who have created speech. But that is only because, being far less intelligent than the

majority of other animals, and more prone to disastrous blunders, in our relationships with others speech is so necessary. (315)

And in a scene that harks back to the Louvinie episode in *Meridian*, Olivia examines an intersection of language and the psychology of oppression:

> If you tear out the tongue of another, you have a tongue in your hand the rest of your life. You are responsible, therefore, for all that person might have said. It is the torturers who come to understand this, who change. Some do, you know. (310–11)

Literary politics is also covered. Olivia contends that by using the Bible to perpetuate slavery, the white man has "spoiled even the most literary form of God experience for us" (147). Ola advances, on behalf of Walker, a thinly veiled addendum to *The Color Purple*. Explaining why he doesn't portray his people at their best, he exclaims, "When my people stop acting like the white man, I can write plays that show them at their best!" (182)

An additional topic for discussion is the shift from oral to written traditions, indeed the tyranny of written traditions. And, of course, there is the not-so-startling series of names to underscore the struggles for dominance that break out all through the novel. Carlotta's father remains silent when he is beaten by his captors. He would never reveal his name to them, so they simply called him Jesús instead. Zedé was alternately dubbed Consuelo, Connie, or Chaquita by the people for whom she worked. She, too, refuses to reveal her true name. Mary Ann Haverstock changes her name to Mary Jane Briden as she is "eager to give up being who I was" (207). Arveyda, who was named after a bar of soap, discovers that the mother he had known as Katherine Degos started out in the world as Georgia Smith. Suwelo began as Louis Jr.; Ola was once Dahvid. Fanny's therapist, Robin Ramirez, uses "Robin" because it doesn't sound Mexican. Fanny Nzingha received her name because "Fanny" represented sassiness and rebelliousness to her grand-mother, Celie, and "Nzingha," the name of a woman who ruled Angola, was seen as a much better middle name than Lou or Jean by her mother, Olivia. And when Shug founds her own religion, it is decided that G-O-D should have no name at all.

The *Temple of My Familiar* is Walker's fullest rendering of the language theme. She hasn't fallen far from Louvinie's ill-fated magnolia.

III

One cannot get very far into an Ishmael Reed novel without encountering commentary or symbolism relative to the role of language in social, political, or cultural struggle. Such comments are essential to the overall development of his work. In fact, in *Mumbo Jumbo*, *Flight to Canada*, and *Reckless Eyeballing*, language assumes the force of main characters.

In *Mumbo Jumbo*, there is in the 1920s an outbreak of Jes Grew, a positive disease that makes folks feel good. Reed describes it as "an anti-plague, enlivening the host, as electric as life, the delight of the gods" (9). Not being among those "germs that avoided words," Jes Grew is drawn toward New York in search of its text, which it needs to attain permanence (36). Without its text, Jes Grew can achieve no more than periodic flare-ups. As the hoodoo detective, PaPa LaBas, expounds: "Jes Grew needed its words to tell its carriers what it was up to. Jes Grew was an influence which sought its text, and whenever it thought it knew the meaning of its words and labanotations it headed in that direction" (241).

Jes Grew's search, however, is fraught with peril. The Atonist's henchmen, the Wallflower Order, seek to suppress Jes Grew and abort the prospect of Jes Grew Carriers in possession of their text shattering artistic norms. The text is eventually destroyed, and Jes Grew does not catch on. The epidemic dissipates, and the Wallflower Order retains control. But the peace is temporary, for in writing *Mumbo Jumbo*, Reed has created another text for Jes Grew and thereby fulfilled a prophecy of LaBas. When asked by Earline if Jes Grew has come to an end, LaBas replies that Jes Grew will return and flourish and that "we will make our own future Text. A future generation of young artists will accomplish this" (233).

In *Flight to Canada*, a novel set against the background of the Civil War, Reed reverses the action. Instead of tracing a search for the text as he does in *Mumbo Jumbo*, Reed constructs a text that is on the move itself. The speaking protagonist is a runaway slave named Raven Quickskill. The skill at which he is quickest is, of course, words. He has written a poem called "Flight to Canada." Then the poem pursues him: "Little did I know when I wrote the poem 'Flight to Canada' that there were so many secrets locked inside its world. It was more of a reading than a writing. Everything it says seems to have caught up with me" (7).

Because the issue of language is germane to the plot, the novel is both vintage Reed and a classic example of African American fiction. Literacy is Raven's liberation: "Raven was the first one of Swille's slaves to read, the first to write and the first to run away" (14). Of course, Swille, the old Massa, has a negative view of Raven's actions, but he also realizes the power of the written word:

> And the worst betrayal of all was Raven Quickskill, my trusted bookkeeper. Fooled around with my books, so that everytime I'd buy a new slave he'd destroy the invoices and I'd have no record of purchase; he was also writing passes and forging freedom papers. We gave him Literacy, the most powerful thing in the pre-techno-logical pre-post-rational age—and what does he do with it? Uses it like that old Voodoo—that old stuff the slaves mumble about. Fetishism and grisly rites, only he doesn't need anything but a pen he had shaped out of cock feathers and chicken claws. (35–36)

In addition to the deeds on the plantation, the freed Raven submits a bill for all of his previous labor, an action that repeats the rite performed by the former slave in Chesnutt's "Tobe's Tribulations." But Raven does far better than he expects. After Swille's death, he eventually returns to take control of the estate. His language skills have served him well.

In *Reckless Eyeballing*, the text has become a play. Raven the poet is replaced by Ian Ball, playwright. This time, the text will make Ian a successful playwright and get him off the sex list compiled by feminists who control the theater. Ian explains his strategy to his mother over the phone: "I've written a play that's guaranteed to please them. The women get all the good parts and the best speeches" (3). Ball does become a commercial success, but the victory is tainted because his compromise has been too great. He lacks the commitment to his own voice displayed by Chorus in *The Last Days of Louisiana Red*.

Chorus, an actor, shoots Minnie Yellings because she talks too much. Chorus has had his lines reduced and his career ruined by hysterical leads dating back to *Antigone*. Nevertheless, he is on the rebound:

> His agent wanted him to fly to New York to check out its dimensions, its acoustics. His voice had been stifled so much over the years through bad distribution, poor and often hostile salesmen, indifference from those at the top that he insisted that a clause be added to his contract giving him the right to satisfactory acoustics. (171)

40

With the description of the stifled voice seeking self-expression, we are on familiar ground. Chorus's flight out of San Francisco is skyjacked, which in itself is of no great concern to Chorus as he readily forks over his money to avoid a hassle. But the voice of Minnie, one of the skyjackers, irks him to no end. She drones on and on, all the while reminding Chorus of his life since *Antigone*, until he can endure no more:

> Minnie moved down the aisle as the men kept an eye on the passengers. She caught Chorus' eye. She paused in front of him. She said she had seen his last performance. She said that she didn't think it was "relevant." She started calling him obscene names, standing in the aisle with her hands on her hips. She went on and on, and every time he tried to get a word in edgewise, she would scream, "YOU LISTEN TO ME, NIGGER. YOU LISTEN TO ME. LET ME FINISH. LET ME FINISH!" Chorus knew what he had to do because he'd be damned if he were going through this scene again. (172–73)

Chorus is more concerned about his voice than about material property or possessions; he is a more serious actor than Ian Ball is a playwright.

Early in *The Free-Lance Pallbearers*, as Bukka Doopeyduk is about to drop out of school, he confers with the dean of Harry Sam College, a figure strongly reminiscent of (though less treacherous than) the Dr. Bledsoe of *Invisible Man* (one of several points at which this novel parodies Ellison's). The dean's name is U2 Polyglot. We can transform this strange moniker to You Are Too Polyglot—that is, one of too many tongues, thereby lacking a strong sense of self. Since his chief activity in the book is pushing around a ball of excrement with his nose as part of his research for a paper on literature, this characterization rings true. Doopeyduk apparently is fortunate not to be swayed by the dean's exhortations to stay enrolled.

Bukka gets married to hen-pecking, lesbian-on-the-sly Fannie Mae and settles down to a life in the Harry Sam Projects, a conscientious worker and disciple of a cult of quixotic do-gooders called the Nazarene Bishops. In the hall of a project building, the following verbal exchange takes place:

> "You must be the couple that moved in here a few weeks ago."
> "That's right. My name is Bukka Doopeyduk. What's yours?"
> "My mother lost my name in a lottery, Mr. Doopeyduk. Why don't you jess call me the neighbor, and so's you kin 'stinguish be-

tween me and my wife, refer to me as M/Neighbor and my wife as F/Neighbor."

"Fine with me," I said. "I have a hard time remembering names anyway." (21)

The projects are compared to prison, the M/Neighbor and F/Neighbor tags being analogous to the numbers by which inmates are officially identified. M/Neighbor and F/Neighbor don't question their misfortune, and Bukka naively helps to perpetuate it. His vision is jaded. To maintain the metaphor, we might say that his tongue is not knowledgeable enough. Only when he finally asserts himself, speaks out, does he assume the role of hero. Unlike the enlightened voice possessed by the protagonist at the end of *Invisible Man*, Bukka's informed voice results in direct social action. His speaking out against Harry Sam brings an end to the Harry Sam regime.

Language also is a major theme in *Yellow Back Radio Broke-Down*. Young rebels—fed up with the same old story, a position their spokesman articulates succinctly—have seized control of the town called Yellow Back Radio, chased out the traditional authorities, and decided to create their own fiction. Drag Gibson spearheads the counterinsurgency, but the Loop Garoo Kid, the hoodoo cowboy who is the novel's hero, helps to secure a win for the new generation. It once emitted signals so faint "it seemed that the whole valley would soon be off the air"; now, however, Yellow Back Radio is again on its feet and communicating well (118).

The language theme is not pervasive in *The Terrible Twos* and *The Terrible Threes*, the first two books (Reed's sixth and eighth novels overall) of a proposed trilogy entitled *The Terribles*, but it remains significant. Although the overriding concerns are the presidency, big business, and international politics, the plot involves an impostor Black Peter who throws his voice through an impostor Santa Claus, having Santa criticize the commercialism surrounding Christmas and calling for a boycott. Black Peter, spotted in his earlier role as a sidewalk hustler, is described by an observer:

> The fellow was a ventriloquist. He could talk at the same time as his little dummy who was engaging the crowd in a game of three-card monte. He said that he was a descendant of a slave named Pompey, a master ventriloquist of the Old South who escaped from slavery by throwing his voice. I've never seen anything like it. He could talk and puff on a marijuana cigarette, imitating President Eisenhower, Winston Churchill, and other famous world leaders. He said that al-

though he was an ordinary, insignificant, and barely literate speaker, he was fortunate that someone named Jah made it possible for the Emperor to speak through him. (*Terrible Twos* 25).

Reed also embellishes the tale with several choice tidbits about language such as the California Supreme Court's decision outlawing the naturalist novel and Satan's concern, because he doesn't understand them, about "microbiologists, deconstructionists, New Age Freaks." Satan contemplates opening a new area for these sinners called Jargon City (*Terrible Threes* 147).

With organisms searching for a life-sustaining sacred text; poems chasing poets; consciously manipulative playwrights; authorial comments on forms of fiction; characters named Chorus, Yellings, and Polyglot; a town called Yellow Back Radio; and a ventriloquist on the loose, Reed's stories strongly echo a dominant impulse in the African American literary tradition. They are, in fact, the tradition's most imaginative examples.

WORKS CITED

Baker, Houston. *Blues, Ideology, and Afro-American Literature: A Vernacular Theory.* Chicago: U of Chicago P, 1984.

Benston, Kimberly. "I Yam What I Am: The Topos of (Un)Naming in Afro-American Literature." In Henry Louis Gates, Jr., ed., *Black Literature and Literary Theory.* New York: Methuen, 1984. 51–72.

Busch, Frederick. Introduction. *"Billy Budd, Sailor" and Other Stories.* By Herman Melville. New York: Penguin, 1986. vii–xxiv.

Chesnutt, Charles W. "A Deep Sleeper." In Sylvia L. Render, ed., *The Short Fiction of Charles W. Chesnutt.* Washington, D.C.: Howard UP, 1969. 115–22.

———. "Tobe's Tribulations." In Sylvia L. Render, ed., *The Short Fiction of Charles W. Chesnutt.* Washington, D.C.: Howard UP, 1969. 97–105.

Delbanco, Andrew. "Talking Texts." Review of *The Signifying Monkey: A Theory of Afro-American Literary Criticism* and *Figures in Black: Words, Signs, and the Racial Self,* by Henry Louis Gates, Jr. *The New Republic* (January 1989): 28–34.

Ellison, Ralph. *Invisible Man* (1952). New York: Vintage, 1972.

Gates, Henry Louis, Jr., ed. *Black Literature and Literary Theory.* New York: Methuen, 1984.

———. *Figures in Black: Words, Signs, and the Racial Self.* New York: Oxford UP, 1987.

———. *The Signifying Monkey: A Theory of Afro-American Literary Criticism.* New York: Oxford UP, 1988.

Himes, Chester. *The Primitive* (1955). New York: New American Library, 1956.

Hurston, Zora Neale. *Their Eyes Were Watching God* (1937). Urbana: U of Illinois P, 1978.

Johnson, Barbara. "Metaphor, Metonymy and Voice in *Their Eyes Were Watching God*." In Henry Louis Gates, Jr., ed., *Black Literature and Literary Theory*. New York: Methuen, 1984. 205–19.

Kemp, Arnold. *Eat of Me: I Am the Savior*. New York: Morrow, 1972.

Melville, Herman. *"Billy Budd, Sailor" and Other Stories*. New York: Penguin, 1986.

———. *Pierre*. 1852.

Morrison, Toni. *Song of Solomon*. New York: Random House, 1977.

Reed, Ishmael. *Flight to Canada*. New York: Random House, 1976.

———. *The Free-Lance Pallbearers*. Garden City, NY: Doubleday, 1967.

———. *The Last Days of Louisiana Red* (1974). New York: Avon, 1976.

———. *Mumbo Jumbo* (1972). New York: Avon, 1976.

———. *Reckless Eyeballing*. New York: St. Martin's Press, 1986.

———. *The Terrible Threes*. New York: Atheneum, 1989.

———. *The Terrible Twos*. New York: St. Martin's Press/Marek, 1982.

———. *Yellow Back Radio Broke-Down*. Garden City, NY: Doubleday, 1969.

Render, Sylvia L., ed. *The Short Fiction of Charles W. Chesnutt*. Washington, D.C.: Howard UP, 1969.

Smitherman, Geneva. *Talkin and Testifyin: The Language of Black America*. Boston: Houghton, 1977.

Twain, Mark. *The Adventures of Huckleberry Finn*. 1885.

———. *The Adventures of Tom Sawyer*. 1876.

Walker, Alice. *The Color Purple* (1982). New York: Washington Square, 1983.

———. *Meridian* (1976). New York: Washington Square, 1977.

———. *The Temple of My Familiar*. San Diego: Harcourt, 1989.

———. *The Third Life of Grange Copeland*. San Diego: Harcourt, 1970.

Washington, Mary Helen. "Taming All That Anger Down: Rage and Silence in Gwendolyn Brooks's *Maud Martha*." In Henry Louis Gates, Jr., ed., *Black Literature and Literary Theory*. New York: Methuen, 1984. 249–62.

Tucept HighJohn
and the Limits of
Language Programming:
A Coda

ARTHUR FLOWERS TAPS OUT, in *De Mojo Blues*, a tale of post-1960s stagnation. His chief concern, socially, is the collectively weak soul of the African diaspora, and his attempt, artistically, is to paint a vision of ultimate triumph. He forges a modern myth out of African American culture, particularly relying upon the hoodoo aesthetic, which is personified most fully in the protagonist, Tucept High-John of Memphis, Tennessee.

The controlling dynamic in the novel is the transformation of Tucept from a disenchanted Vietnam veteran into a hoodoo master selected to deliver "THE CALL" to his people. This drive toward "THE CALL" and the linguistic preparation pertinent to it cleverly mark the novel as one in the African American literary tradition. Moreover, the novel resounds with the blues, the sharp verbal play, and the various allusions to the value of language skill one comes to expect in fiction by African Americans.

Early in the story, as Tucept, upon his return to Memphis, settles into his Riverside Park habitat, he contemplates his postwar existence. His preoccupation with the power of the Word is revealed:

Presented March 5, 1993, at the Graduate School and University Center of the City University of New York at a forum sponsored by the Ph.D. Program in English.

45

Tucept cooled out, lulled by the slow crawl of the river, the water lapping softly at the banks. Old man river. He pulled out Chancellor Williams' *Destruction of Black Civilization* and was soon deep into the ancient glories of Mene's Memphis. Old Memphis on the Nile. Ptah's city, the Egyptian god of scribes. He who thought the world, said it in a word and then it was so. (35)

Tucept has thus, perhaps inadvertently, outlined his own mission: to be a god of the Word himself. But at that point he is unable to respond in full to his calling. Although he possesses some political resolve, he has women to chase, marijuana to smoke, and brooding to do. He finds a river-soaked chair in the Mississippi and spends two years restoring it, often accompanied by the recordings of Lou Rawls. Steadily, albeit slowly, Tucept does move beyond mundane pleasures. He considers more seriously his past and his purpose, an aspect of which is to honor the memory and carry on the work of his late army buddy, Jethro Tree, who first interested him in hoodoo. The Word, naturally, had been at the core of their relationship.

Jethro had inquired about Tucept's surname, which echoes the story of HighJohn the Conqueror, a tale Tucept characterizes as a "slavery myth about some tricking man" (61). This precipitates a rebuke from Jethro, who feels that Tucept lacks proper appreciation of his own heritage. Jethro insists that HighJohn the Conqueror is real and will, in fact, be reappearing soon because African Americans need him desperately. The prophecy is contained, according to Jethro, in the Lost Book of Hoodoo. "Dat's de black book of power," Jethro claims. "De mojo book number one" (61).

There are obviously strong overtones here of Ishmael Reed's *Mumbo Jumbo*. And as Jes Grew must find its text in order to sustain itself, Tucept must locate the Lost Book of Hoodoo to fulfill his potential. The wrinkle that Flowers provides is that the book is not an inanimate text but a hoodoo master named Spijoko who takes Tucept on as an apprentice and teaches him, among other things, that "the Will, the Word and the Way is the whole of sorcery" (87).

Immediately following this particular instruction, when Tucept's sister performs her own version of sorcery, we see a variation on the theme, emphasizing the importance of the Word in the trinity. After years of frustration and financial neglect suffered at the hands of her son's father, who does not acknowledge the child as his own, she torches her ex-lover's luxury car. Caldonia expresses the Will and the Way in the act of arson. But she does not feel completely avenged without sending a note:

> What kind of car was it? [Tucept]
> Deuce and a quarter. Fire engine red.
> Do it Cal.
> It did feel good, she said, sitting across from his whistling with the coffee pot, Caldonia, Caldonia, what makes your big head so hard?
> You think he'll figure out you did it?
> He will when he gets the letter.
> The letter? said a suddenly horrified Tucept, you wrote a letter telling him you did it?
> I couldn't help it. (91–92)

Perhaps Caldonia isn't too wise, but she is certainly in the tradition, providing the word to match the deed. And the episode serves to foreshadow, in broader strokes than Tucept's early invocation to Ptah and Jethro's cryptic prophecy, the course of action to be taken by the protagonist. For Apprentice HighJohn's forte is to be myth, the Word, and his task is to incorporate, through the most advanced type of neurolinguistic programming imaginable, a story of dominance into the souls of people of African descent.

De Mojo Blues is thus linked to what is often called the Whorfian hypothesis, that is, the belief that language shapes, almost exclusively, the way we perceive the world. Allen Walker Read is a prominent exponent of Whorf's position and cites, in turn, the work of Alfred Korzybski to advocate the reorganization of mass character along neurolinguistic and neurosemantic lines. Read warns that correct pronouncements by leaders mean little if not subsequently expressed in the everyday actions of those on the popular level. He argues that through neurolinguistic retraining— brainwashing actually—that end can be achieved.

There are, of course, two major problems with this line of thinking. First, Whorf's position is an overstatement in that, as Eleanor Burke Leacock indicates in "Abstract versus Concrete Speech: A False Dichotomy," Whorf "did not take sufficient account of nonlinguistic cognition" (114). Fortunately, especially since many of us are in reality already being subjected to negative "language programs" on a daily basis (such as the labels some of us have to survive), we are not as language-bound as is generally considered the case. Second, even if we were as dependent upon language as Whorf suggests and susceptible to the type of retraining that Read favors, there could be no consensus reached about who would be responsible for prescribing *the* correct message. Who decides for all whether pronouncements by leaders are, in fact, correct?

Tucept HighJohn, however, will not grapple with such questions. Although Whorfian thought lies at the heart of his own conception (which is also, by the way, a problem with the description of Yaqui in Arnold Kemp's *Eat of Me: I Am the Savior*), he commands power far greater than any social scientist could muster. Through the gift of conjuration, he aims for direct access to and total control over the central nervous system of the Black masses. He will determine all impulses, linguistic and otherwise, present and future. He seeks the limit.

Despite all this movement toward lofty ritualism, the story is kept lively because Tucept remains for most of the novel so recognizably human. He wavers in his commitment to become a hoodoo master, yet he never abandons his work completely. He takes time, as mentioned earlier, to fool around with ordinary things like one-on-one romance. The relationships never work out because, as one may anticipate, it isn't easy for the women he knows to comprehend why he spends so much time pursuing hoodoo. When one of his girlfriends, Lynn, presses him on why he bothers with "mumbo jumbo," he responds that "it's going to get me some sayso" (102). Lynn remains bewildered:

> Some what? She questioned, head cocked off to the side.
>
> Some sayso, he said, voice suddenly throbbing with restrained passion, Some people in this world have sayso, most don't. I want to be one of the people with sayso.
>
> He hated being a bit player in this world, a little man without sayso, helplessly watching his people go down because they lacked understanding of the way of things. (102)

Tucept values nothing above the exercise of his voice, experimenting with the Word. After the break-up with Lynn, and partly because of it, he pursues his studies with Spijoko more intently, closing in on his goal. Finally, as he strides through the park on a stormy day, he creates his masterwork of myth and is ready to program it into the soul of the Tribe. He will take care of genopsycholinguisticide (recall *Savior*) once and for all:

> The saga of the Blacks began to shape itself in his head according to what he wanted to program into the soul of the Tribe. What first, he pondered. Arrogance. He wanted a proud, arrogant

people. He conjured up the first monkey tribes to stand and struggle to humanity and called them Firstborn. Firstborn! To rule is your birthright! He chronicled the founding of civilization, the isolation and sloth of an elder race, the decline of a once mighty people. He built a commitment to the destiny of the race in the Tribe's soul by carving in its conquest and enslavement in hard brutal strokes. He showed the conquest and dispersion of the Folk to the four corners of the earth and called these the Leanyears. We survived.

And then the Longmarches. The Ascension of the Blacks. Tales of relentless struggle and ruthlessly strategic commitment to the destiny of the black generations. Tales of power. Because more than anything he wanted a people bred to the instinct of power. A race of rulers. And so he forged his myth accordingly. A saga of struggle and mastery. The Longmarches. Generations and generations of struggle. Working the Tribe's soul with swift and sure strokes he programmed in traits like discipline and dignity, selfresponsibility and selfdirection, the ability to grow from both victory and defeat. With all the patience of a master craftsman pleased with his work HighJohn carefully weaved an inexorable Will to Power into the soul of the Blacks and exulted in the length of his game. I am HighJohn he howled, and this I swear, the Blacks will never again be enslaved. By the gods and all that's holy I shall forge a race of rulers.

And so into the heart of his myth he placed his survivor's vision. The Blacks still marching where others have long since fallen. Survival of the black generations unto eternity. The Promised Land. His myth came alive, its heart a burning sunheat thing, a beacon in times of both celebration and despair.

The storm around him grew in intensity and he felt its fire in the small hairs of his arm. As he worked he constantly checked his myth for alignment with the Board of Destiny. A good fit. A good Work. He was proud of it. (192–93)

All that remains is for the myth to be planted into the Tribe by means of "THE CALL," the assembling of the masses. Tucept has joined ranks with Ptah himself, has delivered upon Jethro's prophecy, has harnessed and then unleashed, with a Jungian twist, the power of the Word. "I have named the thing and it is done. I am a mighty sorcerer and reality shall yield to me" (215).

Some detractors of *De Mojo Blues* claim that it is an instance in which ideology has hampered craft. They find the closing pages of nationalist rhetoric, as opposed to final dramatic action or concrete expression of the mojo, disturbing to their aesthetics. They wonder, too, why HighJohn is, as Aun Peggy was back in Chesnutt's

Uncle Julius tales, leery about throwing the goopher on the oppressors. If the mojo is so powerful, why can't it be put to immediate political ends? But despite these criticisms, and they do have considerable merit, it is clear that Arthur Flowers has made a stunning contribution, extending, in one sense, the language theme in African American fiction to its logical conclusion. He has absorbed and magnified the sociolinguistic impulses of his predecessors. Think of Harriet Wilson's Frado, coming into her own only when she recognizes the power of her voice to determine, or at least influence, social arrangements; the runaway slaves in the work of Chesnutt and Reed submitting invoices to their ex-masters for services rendered; Janie's struggle, at the heart of Hurston's *Their Eyes Were Watching God*, to become more than a voiceless ornament; Fred Daniels, Richard Wright's underground man, lacking the language to survive; Ellison's Invisible One, described as possessing more big words than a pocket-sized dictionary, hoping to ascend a mountain of words to the top of the Brotherhood; Langston Hughes's Jesse B. Semple, constantly quarreling over semantics; the elaborate naming rituals that are hallmarks of the Morrison and Walker canons.

All these Flowers invokes. These writers and characters have played HighJohn to him.

WORKS CITED

Flowers, Arthur. *De Mojo Blues.* New York: Dutton, 1985.

Leacock, Eleanor Burke. "Abstract versus Concrete Speech: A False Dichotomy." In Courtney B. Cazden, et al., eds., *Functions of Language in the Classroom.* New York: Teachers College Press, 1972. 111–34.

Read, Allen Walker. "The Contribution of Sociolinguistics to the Peacekeeping Process." *Et cetera* 39 (1982): 16–21.

Julius and Jesse in 003

FEELING A NEED TO shake things up, flip the script, depart from the skill and drill stuff that transpired in most basic writing courses dubbed ENGW 003, I decided to have students read several stories that deal extensively with the theme of language empowerment. I wanted them to understand that in some respect these stories address their struggles as language users, particularly ones of African descent who had been classified as remedial writers. However, the specific connections between the texts and their lives would be something the students mostly articulated themselves. I planned to provide commentary, but not before the students had given theirs. The main task I set for myself was to be relatively unobtrusive and allow students to do their work.

The first text was "Dave's Neckliss," a story from Charles Chesnutt's Uncle Julius series (I can never get away from Julius). The stories, or frame tales, contain anecdotes about plantation life related by the former slave, Uncle Julius, within the framework of a larger story narrated by John, the male member of the couple that employs him. Julius's purpose for telling a tale is ultimately to secure some advantage for himself. In this instance, he covets the remainder of a ham that John's wife, Annie, has shared with him. Julius begins to weep and spins the story of how the ham reminds

Presented November 18, 1990, at the Annual Convention of the National Council of Teachers of English. The working title was "Using Literature about Literacy."

51

him of a slave back on the plantation who was falsely accused of stealing a ham from the smokehouse, forced to wear the ham around his neck on a chain as punishment, went insane, even imagined seeing ham trees, eventually thought he was turning into a ham himself, and finally hanged himself over a fire he set in the smokehouse. Touched by the story and for the moment, unlike Julius, turned off by the prospect of eating more ham, Annie gives him the rest. Blended into the story are portrayals of plantation life in which attacks on humanity and voice are foregrounded. For example, it is discovered that Dave has secretly learned to read and has been studying the Bible. Naturally, his master is distressed by the news and, in confronting Dave, asks him what he's learned from the Holy Book. Dave replies adroitly that he has learned not to steal, lie, or be disobedient. His master then decides that the Bible hasn't done Dave any harm and quickly invites him to preach to the rest of the slaves. However, after Dave is framed for the theft of the ham, his Bible is confiscated and burned.

In the ensuing discussion, students did focus, as I had hoped, upon the interplay of language, enslavement, and freedom, but not immediately. Initial reactions addressed how difficult the text was to read because it is written in dialect. In fact, as we read the story in class, several students stopped at various points to protest being given work featuring such poor English. They reasoned that, because one needs good English to make it, people like Julius would never get anywhere in life.

I think, for the most part, the students were telling me what they thought I wanted to hear. After all, this was a writing class, always in their view a place to chastise folks about poor grammar. Besides ignoring the author's use of alternate voices, what they hadn't understood in being intolerant of Uncle Julius is that I valued a clear and effective story above Standard English and believed that their efforts to produce acceptable academic writing depended upon the degree to which they could stress elaboration and clarity over the grammar they were so worried about. I pointed out that I didn't have as much trouble reading "Dave's Neckliss" as I had reading some of their papers, a comment they didn't appreciate at first, although they did affirm that walking off with the ham is a measure of how competent a language user Julius is. When asked, none of them thought they were better storytellers than Uncle Julius. A few, though, were bold enough to claim they were his equals.

As the students further explored the story, their responses grew more varied and unpredictable. One student said the story shows that one shouldn't steal and blame others. In other words, what happens to Dave is sad and shouldn't have happened. On the other hand, others suggested that the aspect of the tale involving the framing of Dave is only a minor issue. Some students doubled back to stress how well Julius gets his point across. I think this was partly another case, since I had argued that Julius's linguistic ability is to be praised, of students catering to what they perceived to be my expectations.

The discussion then shifted to how bad slavery had been. After a spell of communal lamenting, one student posed a rhetorical question: how much freedom do we really have? He promptly declared that we (meaning our enslaved ancestors) had no right to read or preach unless it benefited the master. Several of his classmates chimed in. And although I, myself, am ever prepared to speak at length on this theme, I felt there was nothing for me to add in that vein other than to inquire how that understanding may further inform present perceptions. The students, primarily on their own, had hit upon several features I deemed important.

Certain students, not used to this sort of classroom discourse, pressed for a definitive explanation. They were concerned to know who among them was most right, an impulse highlighted during discussion about what Julius had accomplished. A segment of the class perceived Julius as a trickster figure who "got slick" and "used psychology on the white folks." This group became extremely agitated when an opposing faction felt that Julius was not conniving at all. They figured he was genuinely moved by sad recollection to tell the story about Dave and that the truth and brilliance of the story just happened to strike a receptive and charitable chord in Annie. Despite knowing the trickster figure interpretation to be obvious in the wider literary community, I refused to resolve the dispute, pick a winner, because to tell the supporters of the "naïveté theory" that they were wrong would have constituted a setback for both them and me. I had told them that any reading of a story involves subjectivity, and I didn't see how they could maintain faith in this view if I were willing to call them wrong, even though in some way I felt I had to, about the first major subjective response they cared to air in class. Why would they bother again?

The solution to this dilemma was to distribute another Uncle Julius story, an unscheduled action, in order to expand the frame of reference. "The Goophered Grapevine," the first of the Julius stories chronologically, more clearly spells out how beautifully scheming Julius can be. Upon meeting his future employers, who are contemplating buying land that is of special interest to Julius because of the money he makes from the abundant supply of grapes, the cunning former slave tells them a story about how the property is haunted. The story doesn't work as well for him as the one that gets him the ham, but it left no doubt in any of my students' minds that Uncle Julius is an accomplished con artist. The story wasn't read in class, but comments about it were enthusiastically brought to my attention. Those whose prior notions were validated displayed obvious satisfaction. Just as important, the others seemed pleased to have discerned something without being explicitly directed. When I tried to interject new doubt by intimating that perhaps Julius was sincere after all, one could not distinguish between the replies of the two groups. Neither was going for it.

Unfortunately, the class wasn't as committed to its own ideas in essays. Regardless of my warnings against doing so, one third of the students summarized "Dave's Neckliss" and/or "The Goophered Grapevine." Those in this group still assumed their objective to be strictly informational as opposed to being an attempt to link the texts to their own experiences and the world as they knew it. Others went to the opposite extreme, almost totally leaving the texts behind. So, for one student, "Dave's Neckliss" received a two-line mention prefatory to a lengthy indictment cataloging hardships visited upon African Americans by white America. Some, however, did manage to plant one foot in Julius's world and one foot in their own. One writer, for example, reflected upon why a particular rhetorical strategy had been employed:

> I also notice that Julius must have been a extra ordinary man to be able to use something about slavery to accomplish something so simple and a bit funny. I think that most people find slavery something very serious and do not like speaking about it. But for Julius to have actually experience it and used it like that is different. Then may be that is why he used a story about slavery because he knew people felt serious about it.

Another became involved in a comparison of legal systems:

> The story makes me think about justice. Aren't you glad that your innocent until your proven guilty? I know I'm glad about it. Thank God for the justice system. You know I also think about being in the

hot cotton field. Picking cotton. Imagine me saying yes sir, no sir. My master would have lynched me.

Yet another chose to pursue the language angle mentioned earlier by another student in the class:

The plantation owner had punishment on his mind. The owners of plantations knew that learning how to read would give slaves knowledge and with knowledge comes power. Slaves are suppose to be powerless.

As we shared the papers in class, the strongest negative reactions were reserved for summaries (my influence again), and even those responses were by no means malicious. Discussion of the remaining papers was characterized by receptiveness, and students mainly wanted assertions supported by the text. I was badgered somewhat to finally deliver my own, as if an absolutely correct answer were yet in the offing. But I insisted instead that the stories were the sum total of what had been forwarded by the students and still more. And I left the matter at that, moving on to other crucial questions I wanted them to mull over: How much Uncle Julius can you be? How much Uncle Julius do you need to be?

One writer had anticipated me. She began:

Often in our lives, there are changes that occur. We can either use these changes to benefit us or let it go to waste. In "Dave's Neckliss," both Julius and Dave are affected by circumstances around them.

The student briefly recapitulated the story and proceeded to write:

These two characters, Dave and Julius, have similar personalities. They are both free from the shackles that entangled them physically and psychologically; however, they wish to remain in their past situation. This maybe due to the fact that they are afraid of the unknown, since their minds are not yet freed. I can relate to this aspect of the story, since I, sometimes, unconsciously hold myself back from doing something that I can do. I think the key message in this story is to show us how to make use of the opportunities given to us. . . . I consider my college years the primary years of me expressing myself.

I elected to follow up considerations of language power and self-expression by introducing the class to Jesse B. Semple, Langston Hughes's memorable character, who is one of the most astute language users to be found in any literature. Possessing a strong ego, Semple—or Simple, as he is also known—uses his highly polished wit and oral skill to impress his ideas upon others, usually his barroom buddy, Boyd, narrator of most of the tales. Although Boyd is a man of education—"colleged," as Simple puts it—he holds no advantage over the verbally combative Simple and is never able to change Simple's mind. Acquired in rural Virginia, Baltimore, and Harlem, Simple's experiences form a fortress of meaning more than equal to the assault of the academy. Consider his reaction to Boyd's complaint in "Two Sides Not Enough":

> "I thought you'd get around to race before you got through. You can't discuss any subject at all without bringing in color. God help you! And in reducing everything to two sides, as usual, you oversimplify."
> "What does I do?"
> "I say your semantics make things to simple."
> "My which?"
> "Your verbiage."
> "My what?"
> "Your words, man, your words." (214)

Simple is actually putting Boyd on, for he really understands him all along, as one who had witnessed their conversation in "Concernment" would know. After the narrator has paraphrased a line from *Hamlet*, Simple initiates the following exchange:

> "Boyd, your diploma is worth every penny you paid for it," said Simple. "Only a man who is colleged could talk like that. Me, I speaks simpler, myself."
> "Simplicity can sometimes be more devious than erudition," I said, "especially when it centers in an argumentative ego like yours."
> "Of course," said Simple. (152)

Of the Simple stories we read, "Puerto Ricans" generated the most controversy, as Simple asks why the language a Black person speaks, in this case Spanish as opposed to English, leads to more privileges for the speaker. After widespread, almost obligatory observations that race and discrimination are matters central to the story, several students delivered harsh opinions of Simple, accusing him of putting down foreigners and having a defeatist attitude, so hung up on what the system would not allow him to do. These students, who happened to be from the Caribbean and who identified with the Puerto Rican being, in their view, mistreated by Simple, asserted that the story reminded them of how Blacks in the United States discriminate against immigrants from the Caribbean. Some of their U.S. counterparts conceded that this type of discrimination exists but that they themselves were above such thinking and practice. They did venture to add, however, that Blacks from the Caribbean arrive with the conception that they are better than the Blacks already here. After a few heated exchanges (in easily the liveliest, almost too lively, session of the semester), the presence of those who emerged as peacemakers eventually began to dominate. The talk shifted to how all Black people should stick together.

All this was interesting but had little to do with the story. It is fairly easy to demonstrate among the wider literary community that Simple's beef is not with immigrants but with white Americans. I had to postpone illustrating the point in class, however, because I had announced that my only role during class discussions that preceded the next batch of papers would be to answer questions about information—for example, to define the term *Jim Crow*. As I sought to boost student confidence and encourage interpretive risk taking, I would neither introduce comments nor field questions that had to do with confirming or disconfirming student readings. This placed me in a frustrating posture, but part of what reassures me that it was the correct move is the fact that of eighteen papers I subsequently received, none were strictly summaries, and only in one was summarizing still the dominant tendency.

Of course there was a price to be paid for the activities chosen. As noted, there was a misconstruing of texts and (or because of) too much reliance upon personal experience. There was trouble again with appreciating mood, many failing to imagine the pieces as humorous, probably their most outstanding quality. Authorial viewpoint was largely ignored, several students mentioning, in fact, that Simple *wrote* the stories. This recalls a problem encountered while dealing with the Uncle Julius stories. In general, whatever comments John made about Julius were judged by students to be unquestionably true. That Chesnutt may have provided John's appraisals to show the extent to which people like John misunderstand the Juliuses of the world was not envisioned.

So there was more work in reading to do, more stories, some essays, additional response assignments. While comprehending, to be sure, the subjective nature of textual interpretation, I simultaneously maintain that some subjectivities hold richer explanations than others. I want my students as a whole to be able to perform some fuller "reads," which I believe can help them produce better "writes."

Specific writing problems were indeed addressed. For example, I taught the student who wrote about judicial processes that her audience could think some bridging statements are needed between "Imagine me saying yes sir, no sir" and "My master would have lynched me." Perhaps something like "I wouldn't have done it and, therefore, as punishment . . ." I also indicated that because a slave was valuable property, it was unlikely that a slaveholder would have lynched one based solely upon the type of insubordination she described. I almost threw in some remarks about God and the justice system—but I kept those to myself. The key point is that this student did flesh out her paper through continued drafting.

I showed the student who wrote about self-expression (who was in a basic writing class, not ironically, only because she didn't write enough on the writing assessment test) that to write "their minds are not yet freed" is to contradict her previous claim in the same paragraph that "they are both free from the shackles that entangled them physically and psychologically." This student became a stickler for logic, habitually asking me if her sentences "go together."

In conjunction with a push for greater clarity, time was, yes, spent dealing with matters such as inflections, pronoun usage, and punctuation, as related to their essays, with various rates of improvement among the students over the course of the semester. Some will have an ongoing struggle with mechanics; it's part of the process.

The central point I wish to state here is my belief that the writing activities described above were meaningful and successful—both for the students and for me—mostly because students had been given enough incentive and authority through the stories we read and the discourse surrounding them to develop keenly vested interests in their own writing voices within the confines of a writing classroom. A student noted in reference to Hughes's "Promulgations," "The author write about the way he feels about it. He writing about the situation is a lot and a very good way of dealing with it."

Realizing that simply to exercise the voice, to exercise *authority*, can be significant action is a good understanding of what Julius and Jesse, and Chesnutt and Hughes, are up to. The student may have been responding, and in a manner very much as I have, to Simple's comment that "right now I cannot do much, but I can say all." And to begin to say all, for students who have been labeled remedial, is, as my student hints, a crucial achievement.

WORKS CITED

Chesnutt, Charles W. "Dave's Neckliss" (1889). In Sylvia L. Render, *The Short Fiction of Charles W. Chesnutt*. Washington, D.C.: Howard UP, 1981. 132–41.

————. "The Goophered Grapevine." In *The Conjure Woman*. Ann Arbor, MI: U of Michigan P, 1969. 1–35.

Hughes, Langston. "Concernment." In *Simple's Uncle Sam*. New York: Hill and Wang, 1965. 146–52.

————. "Promulgations." In *Simple's Uncle Sam*. New York: Hill and Wang, 1965. 160–64.

————. "Puerto Ricans" In *The Best of Simple*. New York: Hill and Wang, 1961. 216–18.

————. "Two Sides Not Enough." In *The Best of Simple*. New York: Hill and Wang, 1961. 213–16.

LANGUAGE
AND
LEARNING

One More Time for Professor Nuruddin

Yusuf Nuruddin, my brother. Surely the best arrangement is for me to be there at Medgar Evers College to visit your Black Studies courses. But now that I live two hundred fifty miles from Brooklyn, that option is no longer convenient. So, as per your request, I have sent what you need to do justice to the language unit in your classes. I hope you'll appreciate that I treat African American and Caribbean varieties of English together. You may catch some flak for this. As you know, you teach at the college with the largest concentration in the country of Caribbean students with African bloodlines, many of whom insist upon a cultural distinction in every detail between themselves and African Americans. On the other hand, as you are also well aware, African American students on campus haven't always welcomed their Caribbean schoolmates warmly. So expect some tension. But hold your ground, for this is the way to go. And perhaps this current crop is much hipper anyway, past all that jingoism.

My examples of linguistic features are purposely restricted to the sentence level. I feel you can talk well enough about discourse features such as call-response, talking sweet, toastin', and so on. If not, we can consult some more sources. That analysis is never as complicated as the syntactic stuff, and I imagine it would be more interesting for you to read.

You may get to repay this favor, as I may need a good socio-logical and historical analysis for an English class soon, you know, with new historicism and all. I'll call.

OVERVIEW

Certain language varieties spoken by African Americans and Afro-Caribbeans have often been termed "Broken English" by teachers, students, and the general public. The underlying assumptions are that the language varieties in question are unsystematic, inferior, and the direct cause of poor reading and writing. Nothing could be more inaccurate. These language varieties are rule-governed systems that have developed as a result of conflict, conquest, and cultural mixing. They are equal in a linguistic sense to any other varieties of English and are not a major obstacle to literacy.

ORIGIN AND DEVELOPMENT

Just as English grew and changed because of the Anglo-Saxon invasions, the Danish raids, the Norman conquest, and class divisions within Great Britain, the language changed again when it was exported overseas. Because of British colonizing activity in the New World accompanied by the mass importation of African slaves, the dialects, to use the most familiar label, spoken by most African Americans and Anglophone Caribbeans represent a merging of some aspects and practices of English and several languages of Africa. Although it was standard procedure to mix slaves from different groups together in an attempt to stifle their verbal inter-action, some degree of verbal communication among them was necessary for plantations to operate effectively. In addition, masters and overseers needed to be able to address and receive reports from their workers. To accomplish these ends, new language varieties were created by combining what appeared to be the simplest (which usually meant least redundant) elements of two or more existing languages. Such newly created language systems are called *pidgins*.

In time, children are born who acquire a pidgin as their first language. The language combination is then said to have *creolized* and is referred to as a *creole*. People from the Caribbean sometimes say they speak Creole, which is true, but they are really talking about a particular creole, as *creole* also functions as a generic term. Jamaican Creole, for instance, also known as *patois*, is indeed a creole. But so are the range of dialects we generally call Black English.

The language varieties being considered can all be classified, following the lead of John Holm, under the heading *Atlantic Creole*, *AC* for short.* Creoles basically contain the syntax of the language of less or least prestige and the lexicon of the privileged tongue. AC, then, is an amalgam of English and structures from several African languages. But proportions are not absolute. Some brands of AC are closer to Standard English syntax than others, and African lexical items have been incorporated into Standard English. Words borrowed from Africa include *yam, tote, gumbo, gorilla, elephant, okra, jazz, oasis, sorcery, cola, banana,* and *banjo*.

The above view of language formation is known as the *creole hypothesis* and is the explanation for AC given the most credence by contemporary linguists. Competing claims that AC symbolizes cognitive deficiency, or attests to physiological differences, or derives from white regional speech, or mostly signifies an evolution of Portuguese trade pidgin lack compulsion.

Creoles change over time, as all varieties do, usually moving closer to the dominant language. This is *decreolization*. Language varieties can also *recreolize*, that is, move in the opposite direction. It all depends upon social activities at large. That African Americans have been a numerical minority in the United States accounts for the great degree of decreolization in this country. Differences between AC in Jamaica and Barbados result largely from different histories of colonization and economic organization. Jamaica, for example, was ruled by Spain, then Britain, and housed large sugar plantations with relatively high slave-to-master ratios, while Barbados, "Little England," was never colonized by anyone but Big England and featured mainly small farms and low slave-to-master ratios.

Geography also accounts for differences. Jamaica, after all, is one thousand miles from Barbados, roughly the distance from New York to St. Louis. Usage is also influenced by gender, class, education, attitude, age, degrees of assimilation, contact with languages other than English, and so on. AC will vary slightly, therefore, from nation to nation and within nations, similar to how Standard English varies from Australia to New Zealand and from New England to Texas. What must be stressed, however, is AC's essential character. Despite differences among varieties, their similarities are

*Atlantic Creoles also include those based on other dominant languages like Dutch, French, and Spanish. For convenience I limit the term's use to English-based creoles.

far greater. They don't vary as much from one another as they do from Standard English. As J. L. Dillard points out, "the English of most American Blacks retains some features which are common to both Caribbean and West African varieties of English" (6).

LANGUAGE FEATURES

The following examples come from speech samples or student essays. The country where each subject spent his or her formative years is noted in parentheses. Although I approach them from the angle of inflections and spelling, there are other classification schemes for discussing syntax and phonology issues. I am not attempting an exhaustive or theoretically sophisticated review. I wish to keep this both condensed and useful.

Inflections

Inflections are changes in word form that indicate how a particular word is being used. For example, in the statement "We are interested in Malcolm's ideas," the *'s* is a suffix that completes the possessive construction. Generally, inflections proliferate when word order is relatively unimportant. That is why English, centuries ago, deriving mainly from German, had many noun and verb inflections. Word order wasn't an overriding feature of the language then. It since has become so. Subject, object, and possession can all be demonstrated by word order, and inflections are not needed to convey meaning—the reason, in fact, many have become obsolete. Even the distinction between *who* and *whom* is weakening and perhaps disappearing.

Inflections were not a feature of West African languages, and in the merger of those languages with English, inflections, being unnecessary to making meaning, did not become a significant feature of the creoles. Speakers of AC systematically eliminate certain redundancies relative to nouns, pronouns, and verbs. Instances commonly described as subject-verb (dis)agreement, tense, pronoun, or possessive errors are directly tied, as illustrated below, to this practice.

1. *She have* a Benz that she and Carl call the Status Symbol. (Guyana)
2. When *a young child have* a baby she is not ready for, problems come. (Guyana)
3. *A student do* have some say in the matter. (Jamaica)
4. *He need* to get with the program. (U.S.A.)

5. *Blacks* in South Africa *is refused* decent health care. (Barbados)
6. *He play* four instruments. (Trinidad).

No doubt, these types of constructions irk more than a few speech and English teachers, many of whom would be quick to assert that the speakers or writers don't know grammar or, even worse, that the sentences make no sense. But these configurations result from the application of a specifiable rule, in this case that only one form of a verb be used with all subjects. In an absolute sense, these constructions are no less meaningful or more ambiguous than their Standard English translations:

7. *She has* a Benz that she and Carl call the Status Symbol.
8. When *a young child has* a baby she is not ready for, problems come.
9. *A student does* have some say in the matter.
10. *He needs* to get with the program.
11. Blacks in South Africa *are refused* decent health care.
12. *He plays* four instruments.

The substitutions of *has* for *have*, *does* for *do*, *needs* for *need*, and *plays* for *play* don't clarify the statements. That the latter forms indicate singularity is true, but they don't create it. A *student* and *a young child* would not be confused with plural forms by any native speaker of English. To inflect a verb to show singularity, plurality, or person is redundant because the subject alone denotes these attributes.

AC speakers will sometimes produce forms like *they does* because they are struggling with conflicting rule systems. This is called *hypercorrection.* Hypercorrect forms are actually incorrect in all varieties of English. It is the same type of overgeneralization committed when a speaker learns how to indicate past tense but says *he goed* instead of *he went.* An additional example:

13. Sometimes in life we experience certain *things that tells* us we have to make a decision. (Guyana)

As stated previously, speakers of AC often do not mark for tense:

14. I was on my own. 15. It was very hard because I *have* to work day and night. (Jamaica)
16. Back when I was fourteen, I *drop* out of school. (Antigua)
17. Most of the factors *mention* about teenagers in my paragraphs are trends followed by most teenagers today. (Grenada)

18. I finally got away from my family. 19. Then I *start* having children right after I got married. (U.S.A.)

One would be justified in saying, to the horror of many language guardians, that AC represents an advanced variety of English, historically speaking, particularly with respect to verb usage. As Frederic Cassidy explains:

> Those of us who were brought up on Latin Grammar sometimes do not realise that the Standard English verb today has only three living inflectional suffixes: *(e)s* of the third person singular (*goes, sings*), *(e)d* (or *t*) of the weak past (tast*ed*, swep*t*) and *ing* of the present participle (com*ing*). One cannot even include the *(e)n* of such verbs as brok*en*, since it is never added to new verbs, and survives in a decreasing number of old ones. In the course of its history the English verb has been discarding inflection more and more. (57–58)

AC varieties of English assign a fixed form to nouns, usually the Standard English singular. Thus, we obtain the following:

20. Teenagers especially in America have the attitude of separating most *adult* from them. (Grenada)

21. Especially in those high technology *continent* such as America and Europe. (Grenada)

22. The hard facts hit us about a few *week* later when we had to start finding jobs to support ourselves. (Jamaica)

Hypercorrect utterances include:

23. I did not think *an adults* could say much.

One form of a pronoun is generally chosen or repeated. The subject pronoun may serve as the possessive pronoun also:

24. They still don't think that we are *they* equal. (Barbados)

25. They better bring *they* best! (U.S.A.)

Sometimes the Standard English subject pronoun becomes the object pronoun. Instead of *her* and *they*, we get:

26. Look at *she*! (Trinidad)

27. There are too many young people having babies and *them* themselves are still babies. (Guyana)

Along with possessive pronouns and "apostrophe *s*" (*town's people*), possession is indicated in Standard English by preposition (*people of the town*) or by juxtaposition (*townspeople*) Speakers of AC rely almost exclusively on juxtaposition:

28. *My parents business* was about to collapse. (Jamaica)

The convergence of AC pronunciation and the redundant aspect of all inflections determine the nature of auxiliary constructions:

29. This *has strengthen* me to be an example for my peers. (Trinidad)
30. But where his kids *were concern*, nothing was too strenuous for my dad. (Trinidad)

Hypercorrect forms produced include:

31. But he *did not succeeded* in doing so. (Jamaica)
32. This *could indicated* that this area was new to her. (Guyana)

Spelling

Anyone can have trouble with words that sound alike. Speakers of various English varieties confuse your/you're, no/know, to/too (and even two), and there/their. One can, of course, add other examples. Speakers of AC share the potential for these problems, and, because of pronunciation rules of AC, they have additional sets of homophones. Influenced heavily by the phonology of West African languages, speakers of AC soften consonant clusters at the beginning and end of many words. The initial *th* sound, for example, becomes *d* or *t*. So, where *taught* and *thought* are not homophones to speakers of Standard English (in this case, not for speakers of the U.S. creole either), they are to many speakers of AC. Sentences like these are written frequently:

33. Fred wrote an essay he *taught* was excellent. (Grenada)
34. One must be *thought* responsibility. (Trinidad)
35. The kids who were being *thought* by Miss Moore didn't have much pride because of their environment. (Trinidad)

Although the softening of the initial *th* is only one of many AC phonological rules, it receives a lot of attention because initial *th* is a feature of many of the most commonly used words in English.

The softening of final consonant clusters also creates homophones specific to AC. For example: *mine/mind, fine/find*:

36. I really wouldn't *mine* having an Acura Legend. (U.S.A.)
37. In the 1980s you will *fine* more people having sex than in the 1960s. (Guyana)

Among AC speakers, Jamaicans possess a distinct feature:

... *h* behaves in a non-Standard way. It is, as often as not, prefixed to stressed vowels or diphthongs, as in *heggs* and *hice*, and dropped irregularly from other words—*'ow, 'igh, 'ouse.* This is very much like Cockney usage—indeed, some historical connection is not at all impossible; yet the Jamaican and Cockney confusions with *h* may merely result from the same conditions: loss of the sound, followed by an attempt to replace it that goes awry and puts it in the un-Standard places. (Cassidy 36–37)

EDUCATIONAL IMPLICATIONS

I promise not to take you too far afield here, but I think it's important to indicate the major camps in terms of dialect and education issues. I term them *eradicationists, bidialectalists,* and *pluralists.*

The eradicationists would argue that schools should attempt to eradicate AC because it represents deficient speech and interferes with the acquisition of Standard English. But while linguistic variation can contribute to minor problems of reading and writing, it is not the major cause of reading and writing problems. (Remember, dialects of English are far more alike than they are unalike.) Grapholects (writing systems) bridge dialects, which is why people from various English-speaking regions can read common texts in Standard English, or even in dialects such as AC. People don't read solely the way they speak. Nor do they write the way they speak unless they draw only upon native oral resources. To develop a Standard English "writing voice" is the key, and that comes through continual and plentiful practice by motivated students, not through drills aimed at eliminating the vernacular. To spend time on eradicationist attempts, given the badge of identity that language is, invites cultural resistance that hampers, perhaps even dooms, instructional efforts. This is not to argue that teaching Standard English, the language of wider communication, is never a legitimate school goal, only that it is not likely to happen through a policy of eradicationism.

Pluralists would maintain that most of the educational problems encountered by speakers of AC stem from who they are, not which language variety they utter. They understand that AC and Standard English are linguistically equal and know that the fact that they are not equal in society is a matter of society, not linguistics. The crucial work for pluralists is expressly political: shake up school and society so language variation doesn't play out so negatively in classrooms. Get AC some real respect, some acceptance.

Pluralists wouldn't ignore Standard English, but they do feel that in a more equitable societal arrangement and school situation, students generally would want to expand their use of Standard English and, in fact, do so very well.

Bidialectalists know what pluralists know, namely that AC is not inferior to Standard English in a linguistic sense. However, they would make the seemingly pragmatic argument that AC speakers will need Standard English to succeed in the mainstream. Theirs is an accommodationist strategy: they don't want to make much of a fuss.

I'm down with the pluralists. Educational initiatives that fail explicitly to consider or address social relations and student perceptions are impoverished in my view and are geared to fail students, like many of those of African descent, who feel reasons not to melt on into the program.

I'll stop for now. You easily have one whole class period covered. Maybe two. And you can assign field work.

WORKS CITED

Cassidy, Frederic G. *Jamaica Talk: Three Hundred Years of the English Language in Jamaica* (1961). London: McMillan Education, 1982.

Dillard, J. L. *Black English: Its History and Usage in the United States* 1972. New York: Vintage, 1973.

Holm, John A. *Pidgins and Creoles: Reference Survey*. Cambridge: Cambridge UP, 1989.

_____. *Pidgins and Creoles: Theory and Structure*. Cambridge: Cambridge UP, 1988.

Smitherman, Geneva. *Talkin and Testifyin: The Language of Black America* (1977). Detroit: Wayne State UP, 1986.

LANGUAGE LEARNING
AND
DEMOCRATIC DEVELOPMENT

I HAVE SOUGHT TO AVOID hopping from one bandwagon to another, a behavior characteristic of American educators. My decisions to embrace or reject phonics or teaching grammar or back-to-basics or process writing instruction or critical thinking courses have not been based upon the shrillness or popularity of rhetoric but upon cautious consideration of practice and theory. As I have argued, often in a winding and inductive way, in favor of pluralistic educational initiatives, against monocultural ideals, in favor of emphasizing literature in basic writing courses, I have been approaching, sometimes unwittingly, a deductive vantage point from which I can efficiently analyze educational proposals. This viewpoint mainly entails a concern with democratic schooling and affords an extremely useful typology: either educational proposals promote democracy and thus are to be favored, or they do not. This is how I am viewing language arts learning proposals for all levels, including adult education programs.

Let me confess at this point, while I'm being purposely political, that a small part of me leans toward benevolent dictatorship as the superior form of government. I believe it was Sartre who asserted that when one chooses, one chooses for all, and I take those

Presented December 9, 1992, at the Graduate School and University Center of the City University of New York, as part of the Distinguished Speakers Series in Adult Learning sponsored by the CUNY Office of Academic Affairs.

words too literally at times, as I'm sure Sartre would discourage. At any rate, since I would never trust any dictator to be totally beneficent other than myself, the greater part of me sees true democracy as our nation's best hope. If we're not struggling toward that as educators, we're not struggling toward anything worthwhile.

Our work as teachers is political—whether we construe it that way or not—and our obligation, which we sometimes shun, is to provide clarity of political vision regarding our teaching endeavors. My vision yields the following mission statement: literacy educators further the development of authentic democracy—enlightened citizenry and all that—by helping to create informed, critical, powerful, independent, and culturally sensitive student voices.

Of course I'm not pretending to be original. Thomas Jefferson knew the value of heightened dialogue and asserted more than two hundred years ago that given a preference, he would choose newspapers without government rather than government without newspapers, although Jefferson may have softened that stance somewhat had he been around to watch newspapers beat up Gary Hart and Bill Clinton or to discover how susceptible to propaganda, especially in the television age, many Americans have become. There can be no democracy in the full sense he envisioned without universal, critical literacy. This condition does not exist in our society and is why I have been qualifying the term *democracy* with descriptors like *true* and *authentic*. Because Jefferson was a slaveholder, he was more than a little bit hypocritical, but his better notions, like his understanding that governance by internal authority requires widespread informed debate, are yet worthwhile.

John Dewey took this conception a step further. In *Democracy and Education*, which appeared more than eighty years ago, he wrote:

> A democracy is more than a form of government; it is primarily a mode of associated living, of conjoint communicated experience. The extension in space of the number of individuals who participate in an interest so that each has to refer his own action to that of others, and to consider the action of others to give point and direction to his own, is equivalent to the breaking down of those barriers of class, race, and national territory which kept men from perceiving the full import of their activity. These more numerous and more varied points of contact denote a greater diversity of stimuli to which an individual has to respond; they consequently put a premium on variation in his action. They secure a liberation of powers

which remain suppressed as long as the incitations to action are partial, as they must be in a group which in its exclusiveness shuts out many interests. (87)

Paulo Freire also develops this idea of culturally diverse stimulation, while examining more directly the relative positions of students and teachers. In *Pedagogy of the Oppressed*, which appeared more than twenty-five years ago, he asserts:

> A careful analysis of the teacher-student relationship at any level, inside or outside the school, reveals its fundamentally narrative character. This relationship involves a narrating subject (the teacher) and patient, listening objects (the students). The contents, whether values or empirical dimensions of reality, tend in the process of being narrated to become lifeless and petrified. Education is suffering from narration sickness. (57)

There was enough of a Jeffersonian-Deweyan-Freirean strain kept alive among language arts professionals to bring about the English Coalition Conference of 1987, convened in a nation probably more diverse and booming with more narration than could have been predicted by these intellectual antecedents of the conference participants. At the gathering, the theme of which was "Democracy through Language," old ideas were reworked and invigorated. An excerpt from the conference report reads:

> The increased heterogeneity of our society also gives new urgency to enhancing students' ability to appreciate cultural diversity and multiple ways of reading and writing. The information explosion makes learning how to read and write absolutely vital for living, because without these abilities students will not be able to assimilate, evaluate, and control the immense amount of knowledge and the great number of messages which are produced every day. The development of new media similarly requires of citizens an enhanced ability to use different ways of reading and writing, and language arts instruction has an important role to play here. (86)

Perhaps no students have been more shut out, objectified, and bewildered than those who eventually enroll in adult education programs or those who enter so-called remedial programs in open-admissions colleges. These two groups can reasonably be viewed as one in some respects. I have, in fact, seen students proceed from adult education programs into colleges as discretionary admits, meaning without high school diplomas, and subsequently be referred back to adult education programs. The important matter is that most of these students have not prospered in our system of public education.

Many adult education students are members of ethnic minority or immigrant groups, of a people whose numbers on these shores are tied directly either to bloodshed or to dreams. When we meet them, they have not given up hope of securing credentials that will, they feel, enable them to succeed. Unfortunately, however, a large percentage of these students (like too many students overall) will be subjected to instructional practices that will not help them toward their goal. They are eager yet passive, maybe the worst disposition, in the long run, any group of students can possess. They search for saviors, instead of guides, in teachers, many of whom all too willingly accept the role. These students search for magic in methods; they settle for getting taught at while they fail to see themselves as largely responsible for their own learning. And what is especially ironic and painful to realize, as a spectator to some of this educational parade, is that these students' lives in many instances are the very case studies that indicate the ineffectiveness, from the standpoint of their own benefit, of dictatorial teaching. They indeed suffer—they, not education—personally, not abstractly—from narration sickness. And we lose them again.

I always hope to get in my class students who have been rather rebellious in previous schools and who prove to be somewhat contentious in general. I want to work with these spunky souls, who often not only know where they want to go (which most students know at least vaguely) but may have some strong and sensible ideas about how they want to get there. But, alas, I don't start out with these nervy types very frequently. I see instead remedial students doing the good old remedial thing, waiting on the remedy. They are expecting isolated, prepackaged grammar lessons. They are waiting on presentation of written format divorced from ongoing reading. I have had basic writing students ask me why I put so many reading assignments on the syllabus. After all, they reason, ever mindful of their convoluted prose, they have taken the course to learn how to write. And they are almost hopelessly intimidated by literary texts. I'll stretch this last point out a bit further, for I think that attempting to resolve the problem indicated here is perhaps the most important work I have done in class.

Several years ago, when reading essays students had submitted after reading a William Faulkner short story, "Dry September," I encountered a startling beginning: "This story was written in 1931 on a hot dry day in the month of September."

I was taken aback because a hot dry September day is simply the backdrop *in* the tale, and 1931 is the publication date indicated on the opening page of the story as it appeared in the anthology. The student demonstrated no understanding of a writer's ability to use language to create a world. In her mind Faulkner was doing the work of a stringer, and she was content to summarize what she perceived to be his impartial recording of events.

When I shared my own reading of "Dry September," a story on one level about a rumor of rape, I started explaining how it spoke to me about a certain psychosexual sickness that lies just below the surface of Southern life easily exposed by even the slightest suggestion of black-on-white rape and how the description of aridity illustrates that sickness. This same student interrupted me. Peevishly she inquired, "Where did you get that from?" She wasn't challenging my originality; she didn't understand my symbol making. Prepared to scour the text for literal evidence, for some words she had missed, she failed to see that an examination of my belief system was more appropriate if she wished to know the total sources from which I derived meaning. Despite my subsequent request for interpretive papers, she penned one of the most detached efforts ever given to me in an English class. Indeed, she was far more concerned with her usage—which, no surprise to me, was poor—than with interpretation. This was a Freshman English class, not a basic writing course, mind you. She had passed one of those already.

Although the most memorable case of what I call low literary self-esteem, this student's plight is not uncommon. A number of students have, like her, staggered through watered-down basic skills or adult education courses only to be left with little or no conception about how to proceed successfully in, say, College English I. This episode helped to convince me that work in literary response should be a mainstay of all reading and writing courses I teach, basic and developmental classes as well as those designated Freshman English. But I still didn't have a broad view, not anything like a theory of democratic schooling. I saw myself as simply making a reasonable response to an immediate problem. As a practical matter, I figured, if students could write critical papers on literature, they could fulfill their English course requirements. The

sooner they started working toward that goal, the better. Addressing the question of teaching literature, Peter Roberts writes:

> One answer to this argument is that in the teaching of Appropriate
> and Effective English, because people have always drawn on the
> techniques of persuasion inherent in the language of written litera-
> ture, the study of written literature is the most fertile ground for
> understanding language use. In other words, the traditional cate-
> gories of literature study—theme, structure/plot, style, content, pur-
> pose—are the very same factors that govern Effective English.
> Therefore, where once literature was an objective in itself, whose
> appreciation was aided by knowledge of its constituent factors, it can
> now also be treated as general exemplification of factors which are
> used in specialized forms of persuasion (i.e. in advertising, labels,
> newspaper articles, etc.). (*West Indians and Their Language* 201)

Influenced by the work of James Britton, through his book
Language and Learning and such essays as "The Role of Fantasy"
and "English Teaching: Retrospect and Prospect," I became
acutely aware of the possibilities of using literature as a way to expand students' conceptual powers and to foster expressive ability.
Naturally, I held a vague notion that it had worked that way for
me. Literature has always been a powerful way of reminding me
that I am not just in the world but of it. Writing about literature or
attempting to compose some myself makes up the bulk of the scrib-
ing I have managed. Through the realm of literature, it can be
argued, runs the clearest path to proficiency in both reading and
writing. In the wider world, stories engage people much more
deeply than drills or restricted assignments, a relationship that
should also hold in educational circles provided students are given
a proper forum.

I came to recognize that the problem with students like the
one who summarized the Faulkner story is not that they are totally
devoid of critical ability. However, because they have learned to be
intimidated, they usually don't bring what are at times substantial
evaluative talents into the arena of formal education. They don't
cope well with the surprising experience of being asked to pass
judgment on texts already certified as great works, or so it appears,
signified by their presence in an anthology or on a teacher's syllabus. Teachers themselves, sometimes merely by the sureness and
forcefulness with which they speak about a piece of literature, frequently dominate class discussion and give the impression that
their opinion is really the only important one, even as they push

transactional or reader-response theory. I know I have quoted Louise Rosenblatt on the one hand, trying to persuade students that the primary subject matter of their papers had to be "the web of sensations and ideas that they spun between themselves and the text" (*The Reader, the Text, the Poem* 137), while on the other hand becoming too directive of their spinning. Such intrusion short-circuits the interpretive endeavor and fails to lend strength to student voices. Rather than look to deficit and skills models to explain student withdrawal from classroom literary encounters, teachers would do well to examine their own roles during such activities. There certainly are specific strategies that readers at every level can learn to employ to make better sense of texts, but these strategies are not the discrete "skills" about which many reading teachers are concerned. We could introduce teachers themselves to deconstruction, for example, as a critical tool without assuming a skills or decoding deficiency on their part. If we did assume deficiency of this sort, they would be right to feel insulted.

As my outlook broadened, with graduate study and the like, as well as finally and consciously linking political ideas I had held more explicitly to my work, I was able to articulate more substantial reasons for using literature in all language arts classes. I understood that along with passing courses and becoming more literate, it is fundamental that students gain practice in developing beliefs that are to be defended, amended, or discarded as they participate in the discourse of academic and wider formal settings, since informed and powerful voices existing in dialogic and critical relationships is the form of discourse this society supposedly privileges. Other voices, less informed, less powerful, generally are excluded from the dominant societal conversation. I wrote a few years back that surrounding a text in class, being united by it, being at odds with others because of it, approving and/or disapproving it, discussing it confidently, feeling passionate enough to write about it and want to share that writing (which then means attention to conventional usage), seeking new texts, and searching out new talk are some of the most important activities students can undertake—not because they are good ideas in and of themselves, I see now, but because they support democratic development and are on that basis to be favored.

By 1987, I was ready for the English Coalition Conference—if only I had been called. I'm not sure I would have gone anyway. It was held on an old plantation in Maryland, and that's a spooky kind of thing to me. Nonetheless, in my painstaking manner, I had moved very close in spirit to those who participated. To cite another section of their report:

> Teaching students how and why different ways of reading can find different meanings in the same text can provide important experience in understanding and appreciating opposing perspectives. Learning about the many different kinds of writing and ways of thinking which are the subject matter of the language arts curriculum can expand the capacity of students to imagine and value worlds other than their own. The ability to communicate their views in oral and written form and to listen with comprehension to the views of others is also indispensable to citizens in a democracy, and enhancing this ability is a major aim of language arts education. (86)

So neither I nor the folks at the conference would support narrowly defined skills curriculums in adult literacy programs or in any other programs. Interpretive work should characterize the academic lives of students. Reader-response theory, though a step in the right direction, is no miracle cure for all that has gone wrong. And there were no miracles in the class I alluded to earlier. Some students showed marked improvement as critics, while others, including the woman who struggled with the Faulkner story, did not. And even the students who did progress significantly were not as ready for College English II as I would have liked. They were still too afraid of "literature" and not trusting enough of themselves. They didn't display enough of the arrogance that is part of the temperament of all good readers and writers—and viewers, too, I might add, having observed the critical activity surrounding the movie *Malcolm X*.

Some moviegoers pointed out the historical inaccuracies of the film, legitimately so, given that many less informed viewers were ready to accept the film as historically accurate in every detail. Director Spike Lee, equally correct, insisted the film was a dramatic representation of Malcolm's life, not a documentary. As a result, Lee felt justified in taking artistic license. I had no quarrel with any party on this score. In fact, I found this particular debate relatively boring. A more interesting activity for language arts classes is for students and instructors to question how valid the division is that Lee made between dramatic and documentary. Could any film, even a documentary, be completely objective? Or consider *The Autobiography of Malcolm X*, a text regarded as a virtually indisputable source of authority by Lee and many others. Does autobiography have an absolute claim on truth or just a particular one —a subject requesting that we believe the one story of his or her life that only he or she can narrate in first person? I'm not anywhere near commending Bruce Perry's misguided psycho-babble about Malcolm, and I'm certainly not disparaging autobiography as a genre. I wrote one myself. I raise these questions to suggest more ways of talking and getting students to talk about textual authority, maybe to change relations of power between students and texts, to get students to see that they can act powerfully on stories, that stories don't just act on them.

Oprah Winfrey, at least three times on her television talk show discussing Lee's film, implored people not to worry about *Malcolm X*'s length, 201 minutes, but to go see it anyway. I would have liked to hear students talk about why Winfrey felt such exhortation was necessary. To whom did they think Oprah was specifically addressing her remarks? Did they think that a comment was being made about their interests and abilities? If so, what was their response? And what I'd be most interested in regarding any venture involving Malcolm X is what do students, especially adult education students (of whom Malcolm was one), think is the crucial lesson to be learned from his life? Do they accept the weak, tepid line that the central import of his life is that he overcame obstacles and had a tremendous capacity for reinventing himself? I know I don't accept it. You can run to your nearest politician to find a master of hurdling and reinvention. Malcolm stood straight up and aimed a fiery verbal assault directly against white supremacy and economic exploitation. That is what thrilled me on the verge of adolescence. I didn't care that he liked jazz and danced the Jitterbug. I liked Motown and did the Brooklyn Hustle. I didn't care what hard times he had gone through to get to that stance. I had my own hard times to go through. No, what was essential was that he was on the scene by whatever circumstances, tall, majestic, being defiant, and mostly being right. While I am witness to the commodification of X, I'm looking for some X-ification, if you will, some basic decency and far less greed in our structures of commodity. I'm seeking some X-ification, some gentle equalities and student empowerment, in our establishments of education. This is how I am reading X as text.

I may seem far afield from my basic argument, but actually I have merely stepped inside it for a moment, personifying critical reading ability conceived broadly, though, of course, I don't imagine that everyone shares my views or endorses my explication.

Before I begin to wind down, and point out some specific contrasts between authoritarian and democratic practices, I want to be as clear as possible about some of my previous remarks concerning students. I don't mean to imply that all adult education students are so easily victimized or that all programs are set up in such a way as to achieve victimization. Neither do I mean to underplay psychological strategies that account for student behavior, a passive rejection of certain kinds of formal instruction, for example. Nor do I ignore external social factors that undermine success. I simply wish to emphasize what I feel most familiar with, a seemingly enabling eagerness and availability to learn rendered nearly useless in school by a learned passivity about how schooling should proceed.

A view of knowledge as lore, then, as accumulated information, is an authoritarian view. A teacher holding this view would consequently conduct classes in an authoritarian manner, assuming his or her rightful function to be that of distributing knowledge to his or her charges. This promotes the student passivity I have been describing. On the other hand, from a democratic view, knowledge is a process that is only successful in schools with active student participation, which is proper preparation for the active, participatory lifestyles envisioned by some of the scholars mentioned earlier.

The construct that admirable progress is being made as teachers "cover the material" is an authoritarian construct. That more meaningful activity occurs when students "uncover material" is a democratic construct.

To focus exclusively on teachers' purposes is authoritarian. Cointentional education, as Freire puts it, is preferable—not because it has a nice ring to it, but because it is democratic.

A deficit model of language differences is also authoritarian. Deviations from standard or target usage are treated as deficiencies. Black English is "Broken English" and has to be repaired. Jamaican Creole is "Broken English" and has to operated upon. There is a line on the back of the City University of New York Writing Assessment Test booklet on which students are to indicate their native language. Many students from the Caribbean indeed write "Broken English" on this line. The first few times I saw this, I thought the students were being facetious. But I soon changed my mind. The rate at which they were failing the exam was no joke.

Students, not dialects, have been broken, and negative responses to language differences have been much of their problem. An equality model of language variation, the only one supported by modern sociolinguistic scholarship, does not support repair-model instruction. Understanding, as George Bernard Shaw did, that "a language is a dialect with an army behind it," democratic educators focus upon repertoire expansion. They accept the legitimacy of various types of English and study them so as contribute to an enlightened discussion of learning and teaching with respect to the various speaking populations to be served.

I think the history of English, if only in a rudimentary way, is an important topic for language arts classrooms. We could all stand to know how closely the earlier evolution of English was tied to politics and warfare. We could start with the collapse of the Roman Empire in the fifth century, talk some about clashes among Jutes, Celts, Angles, and Saxons, and how this activity led to the development of certain Englishes, as did conflict with the Norse, from whom were borrowed such essential items as the pronouns *they,* *them,* and *their.* We could talk about Duke William and his posse of Normans, their (remember a word from the Norse) conquest causing a considerable "Frenchifying" of English. *Government,* a word central to this presentation, is a French word. Then we have to notice the Anglo-Saxons, back in charge and growing strong enough to export English around the world to become the tongue upon which the sun never set. During this period dictionaries and prescriptive grammar books were produced. Standards of usage were established.

Writing instruction in schools has much to do with standards set by powerful groups. Being able to produce texts that meet that standard may be valuable ability. However, a focus on the standard to be reached, accompanied by disregard for different ways students may try to get there, is authoritarian and disabling. An approach in which the prevailing spirit is to take advantage of varying talents, strengths, and interests of students is more enabling, more democratic.

The final area I want to talk about is *multiculturalism.* I find it a term that obscures more than it illumines when forwarded as an educational concept; at least, that's what my conversations with people have led me to conclude. It is easy enough to argue against a monocultural ideal. To privilege one culture amid the wealth of diversity in this nation is certainly to be authoritarian. To celebrate

83

cultural diversity is sensible. But of what is the celebration to consist? I often hear discourse on multiculturalism reduced to the level of cuisine, a chicken chow mein, chicken fettucini, Southern fried chicken, arroz con pollo kind of multiculturalism. I hear leaders say our nation's strength lies in its diversity, though I don't often hear them articulate why, that the real virtue of multiculturalism or ethnic diversity is that it supremely tests the nation's resolve to live up to the rhetoric contained in its most cherished documents. Will we comprehend the teasing oxymoron near the end of Ellison's *Invisible Man?* To quote:

> It's "winner take nothing" that is the great truth of our country or any country. Life is to be lived, not controlled; and humanity is won by continuing to play in the face of certain defeat. Our fate is to become one, and yet many—This is not prophecy, but description. (564).

Ira Shor, who is on the faculty at CUNY's Graduate Center, posed to me a question: what would college language arts classes look like if we took multiculturalism seriously? The obvious answer is that the content of curriculums would change. It would become more diversified. More and more literature by authors from so-called minority groups would be incorporated, and so on. Again, that's the easy answer. I contend, however, that three other results, usually overlooked, of taking multiculturalism seriously are ultimately more important than mere diversification of the canon.

The first result I'm thinking about is that whole departments would be more serious about multiculturalism. This may seem an odd point to make, since I have already mentioned a diversified canon. But such progressive activity is often confined to only a few members in a department. It becomes someone's specialty. We create a cadre of experts on multiculturalism when, in fact, we should all be striving for expertise. Some usually well-intentioned colleagues are still asking me to, quote, "give them something on multiculturalism," like my name is Mr. Multicultural or something like that, like I'm not just one African American man. I see the term on numerous job announcements these days: "Candidate must have demonstrated commitment to multicultural education." I surmise that the insistence on this quality in applicants is because the employers possess so little of it themselves.

The second result I foresee is that the ethnic composition of classrooms would change, especially in upper-level literature courses. A higher concentration of students from so-called minorities might even become language arts professionals. I'm not sure what the exact effect would be on adult education programs, but it would ultimately be positive.

The third result, most important, of taking multiculturalism seriously is that it would disappear, that is, as a distinct educational concept, at least in the sense it now exists. At present, it is an *ism* that circumscribes the failure to take full advantage of the diversity that has always surrounded us. The United States has been a poly-lingual, multicultural nation since its inception, and if the educational system had reflected this reality all along, there would never have been a need to propose this particular *ism* as a panacea for educational ills. If a multicultural ideal were ever present, it would not have become a special movement. In fact, it may be time for another movement, one that stresses not just recognition of diversity but diverse interaction. This new movement, really an eve-of-the-twenty-first-century update of an intellectual tradition I sketched earlier, would emphasize not just multicultural existence but transcultural dialogue.

One evening in a restaurant, I remarked to my friend and colleague Nancy Lester that with all the new experts on multiculturalism running around, it was a clear signal to stop using the term to explain anything. It was time to light out, as Huck Finn might put it, for other rhetorical territory. I was amazed by the numbers. As I reexamined the program for the annual convention of the National Council of Teachers of English in 1981, the first year I attended, I hardly noticed any reference to multiculturalism, though by then I had heard the term used among literary artists for at least a decade. Of approximately two hundred panels and workshops at the six-day conference, only three were billed as multicultural or multiethnic in perspective, and one of those panels was composed entirely of presenters from Canada. The conference theme was "Sustaining the Essentials." For the 1989 NCTE annual convention, the theme was "Celebrating Diversity." Did I hear someone say bandwagon, that it won't last? We'll see.

Insofar as *multi* means diverse fluidity, it sounds good to me. But where *multi* means distinct, as the fixed tile in a mosaic, I think we have problems. This is one reason I enjoyed Toni Morrison's book *Playing in the Dark*. Her ideas about American Africanism—Morrison's phrase to describe how the African presence in the United States profoundly affected the work of writers such as Willa

Cather, Ernest Hemingway, and Mark Twain—make for good cross-cultural conversation.

It is all before us now. There is a past to draw upon but not to duplicate. What about the golden age of American education when all was fine? Forget it. It never happened. Numerous scholars have argued convincingly that American education has generally focused on producing a highly literate elite and a minimally literate general populace. Never was it the most widely held view among administrators to provide high level literacy for everyone, what business leaders are calling for urgently. It is indeed a new literacy challenge we and our students face, a task we must be equal to if we are to have the most favorable participation in civic and business affairs, if our society is genuinely to become more inclusive and approach its full potential for humanism.

WORKS CITED

Britton, James. "English Teaching: Retrospect and Prospect." In Gordon M. Pradl, ed., *Prospect and Retrospect: Selected Essays of James Britton*. Montclair, NJ: Boynton/Cook, 1982. 210–15.

———. *Language and Learning* (1970). Harmondsworth: Penguin, 1972.

———. "The Role of Fantasy." In Gordon M. Pradl, ed., *Prospect and Retrospect: Selected Essays of James Britton*. Montclair, NJ: Boynton/Cook, 1982. 38–45.

Dewey, John. *Democracy and Education* (1916). New York: Free Press, 1966.

Ellison, Ralph. *Invisible Man* (1952). New York: Vintage, 1972.

Freire, Paulo. *Pedagogy of the Oppressed*. New York: Continuum, 1970.

Lloyd-Jones, Richard, and Andrea Lunsford, eds. *The English Coalition Conference: Democracy through Language*. Urbana, IL: NCTE, 1989.

Morrison, Toni. *Playing in the Dark: Whiteness and the Literary Imagination*. Cambridge, MA: Harvard UP, 1992.

Perry, Bruce. *Malcolm X: The Life of a Man Who Changed Black America*. Barrytown, NY: Station Hill Press, 1991.

Roberts, Peter. *West Indians and Their Language*. Cambridge: Cambridge UP, 1988.

Rosenblatt, Louise. *The Reader, the Text, the Poem: The Transactional Theory of the Literary Work*. Carbondale, IL: Southern Illinois UP, 1978.

African American
in Process

In 1988, LISA DELPIT achieved a masterstroke of irony. Writing in the *Harvard Educational Review*, she broached the subject of silence and subsequently hushed much of the audience she was imploring to speak. Her goal in "The Silenced Dialogue: Power and Pedagogy in Educating Other People's Children" was to initiate or redirect conversations about writing pedagogy and to amplify remarks made in a 1986 article entitled "Skills and Other Dilemmas of a Progressive Black Educator." Although praiseworthy in several respects, especially for an analysis of what Delpit calls "the culture of power," the two-part entry also represented somewhat muddled thinking about writing instruction, which undermined her own aims. She argued, even as she offered disclaimers, that writing-process pedagogy is inappropriate for African American children. Such pedagogy, she vaguely contended, emphasizes fluency at the expense of teaching specific skills, a belief supported by several of her African American colleagues.

Delpit recalled how she had learned writing-process pedagogy as a graduate student at a prestigious university. She declined to name the institution. She also offered that she "never wrote any text longer than two sentences" until tenth grade and suggested that the key to her Standard English literacy development was hav-

Excerpts presented November 17, 1994, at the Annual Convention of the National Council of Teachers of English.

ing her speech constantly corrected and spending hours on writing drills ("Skills" 380). She added that when she employed an open classroom model, her white students from "Society Hill" thrived while her African American students from "South Philly" faltered. And her indictment against process strategy was completed when she revealed that Black teachers who confided in her held the opinion that the method is not for Black children and may even be part of a white conspiracy to keep them uneducated. Her friend Cathy (no last name was given) declared: "This is just another one of those racist ploys to keep our kids out. White kids learn how to write a decent sentence. Even if they don't teach them in school, their parents make sure they get what they need. But what about our kids? They don't get it at home and they spend all their time in school learning to be *fluent*. I'm sick of this liberal nonsense" ("Skills" 382).

Delpit quoted other Black teachers but didn't give even their first names. She did not identify sites, provide detailed scenarios, or dispute the ideas of particular educational theorists. There were several reasons, then, she should have received plentiful feedback. She was clearly open to the charge that she had misrepresented process pedagogy; the issue of substantiation seemed germane as well. There were no formal citations, for example, in the 1986 essay. Perhaps most important, her stereotypical images of African American students and of teachers, both African American and European American, were certainly assailable.

Although she received calls in reaction to her work, Delpit's challenge to process pedagogy did not provoke great public response among language arts professionals. Her ideas weren't featured prominently, say, at conferences of the National Council of Teachers of English, a group with enough deconstructionists, problematizers, "site contesters," other assorted contestants, and multiculturalists to boot, to get a good argument going about almost anything. On the other hand, I believe her articles were passed around frequently. In fact, that's how I got them, delivered with some agitation. So the interest was there, but not the noise.

I was approached by colleagues at convention sites several times, most often during the 1992 NCTE Spring Conference in Washington, D.C., where Delpit appeared on a panel I helped to organize. In rather cautious tones, they would ask me about her writings. Much to their relief, I would express a general disagreement with the articles while acknowledging the valuable insights contained therein. My colleagues would respond softly, carefully.

Of course, what accounted for our muted dialogues were the complexions of the people who had approached me. They were the Euro type. They had been stumped, not intellectually but rhetorically. Delpit had played the so-called race card, positing a variation of the basic argument "I'm Black, so I know what's best for Black kids." Not many European Americans seemed willing to call her on that—not out loud. They thereby avoided a possible nationalistic rebuttal. They didn't want to be called racists for expressing legitimate intellectual concerns. At the 1992 conference, only one person, African American educator Dorothy Strickland of Rutgers University, subjected Delpit's analysis to a degree of oppositional scrutiny. At least, this is what I was told. I was primed to speak out also, but in our session other issues came to the fore, and I decided to postpone airing my criticism.

Delpit had also employed a verbal stratagem of "I didn't do it that way, so it's not necessary." But this tactic lacked the impact of the racialized one, and if it had been the major contention in her essays, they wouldn't have drawn much attention, perhaps wouldn't even have been published. Surely they would have quieted no one.

It has also been pointed out to me that gender was a factor in the silence. Women, the explanation goes, are hesitant to criticize publicly other women because it's so hard for women to gain professional acceptance in the first place. Maybe there is something there, although I never heard any women whispering about Camille Paglia. The more cynical read is that white people weren't going to invest much energy debating methodology for African American children. They would argue the product-versus-process issue among themselves, do their best for white children, and leave it at that. However, I couldn't subscribe to that notion because, as indicated, too much European American traffic had come my way. No, the race card was trump.

What I am angling for, then, is fulfillment of Delpit's original goal, which was to spur as many exchanges as possible about the relevance of writing-process instruction for African American children. I think this is best done by specifying the tenets of such instruction, diminishing suppositions, whether they be racialized or otherwise, that don't address the model presented, and then sending invitations for further discussion that people can feel comfortable accepting. I am not concerned primarily with disputing

Delpit. I don't presume she holds those exact views today. In fact, the reason I have dispensed with the academic convention of writing about her texts in the present tense, as you may have already noticed, is to stress my use of them as historical reference points that merely tip an iceberg of contemporary dialectics about writing-process instruction. I have heard many of the same things she has. I, too, talk with Cathys. I am trying to treat their ideas, those of my wary colleagues in convention halls, and Delpit's also, more seriously than has been the case.

Steven Zemelman and Harvey Daniels, in "Defining the Process Paradigm," provide fifteen concepts that, as they say, "should provide a sufficient definition of the process model of writing instruction" (345). As I talk further about Delpit's work, then, I do so with this list in mind:

1. Teachers who understand and appreciate the basic linguistic competence that students bring with them to school, and who therefore have positive expectations for students' achievements in writing.

2. Regular and substantial practice at writing.

3. Instruction in the process of writing—learning how to work at a given writing task in appropriate phases, including prewriting, drafting, and revising.

4. The opportunity to write for real, personally significant purposes.

5. Experience in writing for a wide range of audiences, both inside and outside of school.

6. Rich and continuous reading experience, including both published writing and the work of peers and teachers.

7. Exposure to models of writing in process and writers at work, including both classmates and skilled adult writers.

8. Collaborative activities that provide ideas for writing and guidance in revising drafts in progress.

9. One-to-one writing conferences with the teacher.

10. Inquiry-oriented classroom activities that involve students with rich sets of data and social interaction, and that focus on specific modes or elements of writing.

11. Increased use of sentence-combining exercises, which replaces instruction in grammatical terminology.

12. Mechanics of writing taught in the context of students' own compositions, rather than in separate exercises and drills.

13. Moderate marking of the surface structure errors in student papers, focusing on sets or patterns of related errors.

14. Flexible and cumulative evaluation of writing that stresses revision. The teacher's written comments include a mixture of praise and criticism, with praise dominating.
15. Writing as a tool of learning in all subjects across the curriculum. (345–53)

No teacher is expected to give attention to every dictum, and the authors resist pushing any particular combination. As they explain: "The danger we face in our field today, and it's now a serious threat, is the idea that there is only one right way to handle a given kid, a given grade level, a given chunk of curriculum, a given element of writing. This is not just wrong; it is profoundly, dangerously, insidiously wrong" (355).

Zemelman and Daniels don't seem to be the ones with whom Cathy was upset. They all identify the same problem, a sort of mindless orthodoxy. But where Zemelman and Daniels blame practitioners for the misapplication of writing-process theory, Cathy blamed the paradigm itself. I have some sympathy for her complaint and for Delpit's representation of it. A little hearsay (I've used some already) and the prospects of a good conspiracy theory always pique my interest. However, both Cathy and Delpit failed to develop the story line. To make all students spend all their time on one aspect of writing—say, the fluency that Cathy commented on—is at odds with serious attempts to instantiate writing-process instruction, clashing, at the very least, with features 1, 3, 8, and 14 presented above. So, while I am definitely willing to accept the word of Cathy and other informants that they had encountered inflexible, insensitive, and racist teachers as well as poorly managed writing projects, I don't, on the other hand, see a need to privilege their vague interpretation of educational ideology. The reasoning most useful for the dialogue Delpit urged would expose the stark contradictions between clearly articulated theory and poor practice.

Also useful would be avoidance of unnecessary binarism and reductionism. In Delpit's 1986 article, Blacks were said to fail in the open classroom and fare better in a more rigid, skills-based curriculum. The same was not true of whites. Although the class difference between "Society Hill" students and "South Philly" students was mentioned, it was not acknowledged as a possible explanation for the performance and attitude of each group. One is led to conclude, for example, that *no* African American child prospers in an open classroom and that *all* white students do. Further

91

essentializing occurred when it was claimed that all African American students were already fluent and that work on fluency functioned in opposition to needed work on skills. That African American children wrote elaborate rap songs is cited as proof of the fluency they possessed. Ignored is the reality that fluency is relative to tasks and modes of discourse. People may exhibit different degrees of fluency in different genres. Operationalizing fluency is, in fact, a skill. I am a far less fluent essayist than rapper. I have to push myself much harder to get the essay work done. I free-write, dismiss conventional structures, really force the issue of fluency at times. I push through the relative discomfort. If I didn't, we wouldn't have this text to discuss.

One more word about raps. Students can write them *in* school, a notion not forwarded by Delpit's informants but one that is consistent with item 5. And they can be helped to become more fluent in that activity. I don't buy the stereotype that they are all fluent rappers any more than I believe that they are all natural experts at singing, dancing, and dribbling basketballs.

The most curious dichotomy Delpit used was to pit Black teachers against writing-process teachers. As she wrote in "Skills and Other Dilemmas":

> Writing-process advocates often give the impression that they view the direct teaching of skills to be restrictive to the writing process at best, and at worst, politically repressive to students already oppressed by a racist educational system. Black teachers, *on the other hand* [emphasis mine], see the teaching of skills to be essential to their students' survival. (383)

In this setup, one cannot be Black *and* a writing-process advocate—quite ironic because that is exactly what Delpit herself was and perhaps yet is. And there are others.

African Americans Janis Epps and Jacqueline Royster endorse writing-process instruction in *Tapping Potential: English and Language Arts for the Black Learner*. Epps, in "Killing Them Softly: Why Willie Can't Write," provides a scathing polemic against the restrictive, she would even say genocidal, skills instruction foisted upon African American youth. More important than skills instruction, in her view, are critical thinking and "respect for their own personal experiences and those of their people" (156).

Royster, less strident but equally committed to the education of African Americans, writes in "A New Lease on Writing" that the current trend toward process-oriented teaching seems to be a key asset (163). However, she does note the inconsistencies that may accompany attempts to enact a process model; nevertheless, she reasons that "there is still the potential for great rewards, especially in the areas of inquiry, problem solving, and revision" (163). Royster concludes, quite significantly:

> The fundamental point to be made is that a process-oriented approach to the development of the writing skills of black students has the same potential that it has for the skill development of other students. If we do move in this direction, what we will have to acknowledge first is that even though black students may be different from other students in a variety of ways, the process of educating them may be essentially the same as the process for students in general. We, then, might be in a position to stop identifying black students as forever atypical and to start concentrating our attention on the pressing battle to determine how children with all of their individual differences learn—and how and when we as educators can intervene positively in the learning process. (166)

African American Carol Lee, addressing Delpit's work, writes in her 1993 publication, *Signifying as a Scaffold for Literary Interpretation*:

> I have some reservations about Delpit's specific comments about composition instruction within the process approach or what Hillocks . . . identifies as the natural process mode of instruction. However, I do agree with the basic thrust of her argument about the need to empower students from disenfranchised communities by teaching strategies that will lead to mastery of particular skills and the need for the research community to listen to perspectives articulated by minority researchers. (151)

So one cannot intelligently deny African American scholars their complexity and their ability to engage theory. They will use what they can and discard the rest, not merely because of ethnicity but because of sophisticated intellects at work. African American educators do want African American students to acquire language skills, but they don't all rule out writing process as a means to that end.

Indeed, Delpit's own sophistication belied her report of her own literacy development and that of those she represented. Anyone who reads the 1988 article knows she understood that any form of language use is a manifestation of personal motivation and social dynamics. Nonetheless, the literacy success she cited is attributed solely to skills instruction. To gain a fuller, more accurate sense of that development, we need a more elaborate account of motivation. Her eyes and her classmates' were on the prize, the sparrow, or something similar. One also wonders what to make of her disclosure that she didn't write texts longer than two sentences until the tenth grade. That can't be a recommendation to defer essay writing by African American students until the sophomore year of high school, can it? One wouldn't think so. What would Cathy say?

Actually, in the 1988 article, Delpit lent a powerful voice to the writing-process movement. In conjunction with the aforementioned analysis of the culture of power, a brilliant treatment in which she cogently argued the need to explicitly teach African American students the linguistic and cultural codes that may enable more effective participation by them in the wider realms of language and power (I recommend it highly), she made several strong statements about writing instruction. She warned, for instance, that "merely adopting direct instruction is not the answer. Actual writing for real audiences and real purposes is a vital element in helping students to understand they have an important voice in their own learning processes" ("The Silenced Dialogue" 288).

This sounds like a combination of features 4 and 5. Delpit added that what she meant by skills was "helping students gain a useful knowledge of the conventions of print while engaging in real and useful communicative activities" (295). I take this to be strong affirmation of feature 12.

Perhaps her most clearly rendered suggestion is as follows:

> I suggest that students must be *taught* the codes needed to participate fully in the mainstream of American life, not by being forced to attend to hollow, inane, decontextualized subskills, but rather within the context of meaningful communicative endeavors; that they must be allowed the resource of the teacher's expert knowledge, while being helped to acknowledge their own "expertness" as well; and that even while students are assisted in learning the culture of power, they must also be helped to learn about the arbitrariness of those codes and about the power relationships they represent. (296)

Having argued both sides of the skills/process debate, Delpit called for an end to it. She blamed the whole thing on academics, presumably white ones, and asserted that successful teachers have not confined themselves to either approach. The call is somewhat on target, but I don't think resolution is so simple. There are people who believe that teaching "decontextualized subskills" is the proper path. I have African American colleagues who teach about parts of speech and parts of sentences because, the way they view pedagogy, those are the building blocks students will subsequently employ to write paragraphs and then, if they make it far enough, essays.

I recently observed a basic writing class being taught by an African American instructor in which the students were doing workbook exercises, taking turns supplying answers aloud. One student, a young African American, had arrived late and had barely turned to the proper page by the time his turn came. Trying to orient himself, he asked the instructor, "What are we doing this for?" He didn't know how wise his question was. There was an uneasy and telling silence until a fellow student explained that the class was preparing for the upcoming writing examination and that the exercises were for that purpose. The questioner, seemingly satisfied with the explanation, replied, "Oh, okay," and joined in. To the extent that teachers pursue skills activity *at the expense of* writing, they function in opposition to the process paradigm. The pedagogical space thus created excludes a skills/process intersection. There is a real reason to debate. Textbook companies, like the one that produced the book used by the students mentioned above, know this perfectly well and are scurrying to get bets down on both sides, a fact I became aware of when a salesman visiting my office, undeterred that I lacked interest in a skills-based book, assured me that his company's process textbooks would soon be available.

Enough of hearsay. As we converse, we should pull all the players out into the open. We need to identify fully all the Cathys and push them to make their critique more rigorous, to point fingers explicitly and compel specific responses. We must honor their experiences but not fetishize them. The value of self-report as argument is directly related to how well the experience is theorized. We must remain hesitant to assign causality to correlation. Skills instruction may have been the breakfast of some champion writers, but we hardly need conclude, as I hope the analogy I have chosen makes obvious, that skills instruction alone *created* their success. We must also hear more, loudly, from the colleagues who collar me in the halls. European American teachers are, after all, going to teach the majority of African American children in the foreseeable future. If they can bear the load of that awesome responsibility, they can carry the weight of helping the skills/process dialogue be as productive as possible, specifying, along with the other participants, their particular perspectives and the grounds upon which they are willing to be persuaded about issues.

The skills/process issue is never going to be decided by strict empiricism. Tightly controlled experiments, for obvious ethical and methodological reasons, cannot be applied to most educational processes. The talk that settles the matter, insofar as talk can, will have to contain marvelously insightful descriptions and high-quality rationales. This is the talk I am trying to promote. African American children deserve it.

WORKS CITED

Delpit, Lisa. "The Silenced Dialogue: Power and Pedagogy in Educating Other People's Children." *Harvard Educational Review* 58, No. 3 (August 1988): 280–98.

————. "Skills and Other Dilemmas of a Progressive Black Educator." *Harvard Educational Review* 56, No. 4 (November 1986): 379–85.

Epps, Janis. "Killing Them Softly: Why Willie Can't Write." In Charlotte K. Brooks, ed. *Tapping Potential: English and Language Arts for the Black Learner.* Urbana, IL: NCTE, 1985. 154–58.

Lee, Carol D. *Signifying as a Scaffold for Literary Interpretation: The Pedagogical Implications of an African American Discourse Genre.* Urbana, IL: NCTE, 1993.

Royster, Jacqueline. "A New Lease on Writing." In Charlotte K. Brooks, ed. *Tapping Potential: English and Language Arts for the Black Learner.* Urbana, IL: NCTE, 1985. 159–67.

Zemelman, Steven, and Harvey Daniels. "Defining the Process Paradigm." In Linda Miller Cleary and Michael D. Linn, eds., *Linguistics for Teachers.* New York: McGraw-Hill, 1993. 339–56.

LANGUAGE, RACISM, AND RESISTANCE

A Legacy of Healing:
Words,
African Americans,
and Power

To claim that "words will never hurt me" is the all-time number one act of denial. Only a person profoundly hurt by words would attempt this psychological maneuver. I have, in fact, been rather adept at the sticks-and-stones competition but have been nicked quite a bit, along with others of my ethnic group, by the master narrative in which inferiority is ascribed to those of darker hues. I plead no special case here. African Americans aren't the only ones who don't fare well in the American script of exploitation—just a prominent example. My aim, therefore, is not merely to highlight the victimization of African Americans but to explore adaptive responses to that victimization along the axis of language. In other words, I am considering the healing qualities contained in the counterstory about language that has been central to the African American intellectual and expressive traditions. I don't argue that language alone oppresses, or that a magic combination of syllables could alone secure full empowerment. I simply choose to pay particular attention to the Word, even as I acknowledge that Word and Deed inevitably interact to shape destiny.

Imagine the first African slaves ever captured by Europeans. As soon as they were called *totally out they names*, they had to know they were up against a different game. They weren't losers in a

Presented November 4, 1994, at the Third Annual Conference on African American Language and Communication at Teachers College, Columbia University.

99

mundane intracontinental conflict; they were to be subjected to the largest program of dehumanization ever seen in the western hemisphere, complete with tales and labels, sanctioned by respected intellects, that rationalized enslavement. *Nigger*, because of the variety of powerful reactions it can spur, and because of the particular history and present it inscribes, remains to this day the most potent word in the American vocabulary.

Although captured Africans were suffering huge losses in the skirmish about self-definition (we did call ourselves Negroes well into the twentieth century), they managed some impressive gains along other verbal fronts. Patricia Turner points out in *I Heard It through the Grapevine*, her fascinating study of rumor in African American culture, that the 1839 mutiny aboard the *Amistad* probably began because Cinque and other Africans believed the rumor that they were about to be literally eaten by their captors. That slavers were cannibals, in more than the obvious metaphoric sense, was an idea widely held by Africans. When Cinque and company made their move, therefore, they were propelled toward their eventual freedom by a specific linguistic form. So, while rumor generally connotes negativity, it has functioned systematically in the African American community, as Turner carefully and brilliantly documents, as a method of protection and resistance. Recent and popular rumors suggesting that there is an ingredient in certain fast-food chicken to sterilize Black males, or alleging Ku Klux Klan ownership of clothing companies like Troop, or asserting that Reebok sneakers were manufactured and/or distributed in South Africa circulate as sites of teaching and survival.

The Reebok rumor even convinced supposed empiricists like my wife and me. The Boston-based manufacturer was, in fact, the first major U.S. shoe company to pull its products *out* of South Africa. But when some folks told us about the South Africa angle, and when we pondered how South African the word *Reebok* sounded, we soon vowed never to buy a pair of Reebok sneakers as long as South African apartheid existed. This really bothered our children. It was:

"Mommy, Daddy, but the sneakers is phat!"
"Yeah, but you not gittin em."

Through dialogue about sneakers, a very powerful channel, we taught our children much about colonialism, the Mandelas, and boycott. And to communicate this most effectively, all we had to do

100

was not purchase a few pairs of sneakers, which cost too much anyway. In fact, when one considers that every other major sneaker company has been hit by a rumor connecting it to the predemocracy South African government or the Ku Klux Klan, one understands that some folk are doing fine cultural work in trying to discourage African American youth, an audience specifically targeted by these manufacturers, from so intently, and sometimes perilously, accumulating so many pieces of overpriced leather and rubber. Health is one of the issues here, and not all the rhetoric can be pretty. As Turner concludes, "like a scab that forms over a sore, the rumors are an unattractive but vital mechanism by which the cultural body attempts to protect itself from subsequent infection" (220).

I'm not trying to start any trouble, but Crooked I, a company that produces malt liquor and fruit drinks, may easily be hit by a rumor. Some brother or sister may notice that the company's juices, whatever the flavor, are packaged in black cans and are available almost exclusively in the African American community. Someone else may notice that the product is produced in North Carolina and then associate it with the Ku Klux Klan. Another may discover the ultimately damning scoop, that is, if you dissect the company logo, the Crooked I, vertically, which you can do, say, by covering half of it with your finger, you will clearly see three K's. Opinion then spreads that in KKK-owned Crooked I products there is a chemical (beyond, but clearly connected to, the alcohol in the malt liquor our youth drink too much of) designed to destroy African Americans.

The grapevine also extends to literature. In his 1967 novel, *The Man Who Cried I Am*, John A. Williams has a character discover a document describing the King Alfred Plan, a "final solution" for African Americans in case of continued racial unrest. Agencies such as the FBI, CIA, National Security Council, Department of Defense, and local police forces are to coordinate their efforts in order to neutralize Black leadership and then "terminate, once and for all, the Minority threat to the whole of the American society, and, indeed, the Free World" (372). This conspiracy theory grabbed hold of the mass Black imagination. Black folk skipped past the first twenty-seven chapters to get to this King Alfred Plan they had heard about. They didn't care anything about Harry Ames or Max Reddick or Marion Dawes. The Black Topographical Society based a three-hour political awareness session, one I sat through in the early 1970s, on a version of the proposal. Speakers would explain, for example, that superhighways like the Dan Ryan Expressway in Chicago were always routed through Black ghettos to facilitate eventual military operations against those communities. I told one of the presenters that the King Alfred Plan came out of a novel. He replied that the novel was just telling the truth. And it is certainly easy to comprehend why it could ring true for anyone who had witnessed the suspicious assassinations of Martin Luther King, Jr., Malcolm X, and a long list of others, and who had seen or been a part of the post-Watts wave of inner-city uprisings.

Although it provided ample grist for the rumor mill, Williams's novel is, in addition, firmly linked to texts in the African American literary tradition. The Wright-like figure Harry Ames asserts, "I'm the way I am, the kind of writer I am, and you may be too, because I'm a black man; therefore, we're in rebellion; we've got to be. We have no other function as valid as that one" (49). The story is—as most stories in the tradition are—largely about the tension between expression and repression of the Black voice. This dynamic is manifest, for example, in the very first novel by an African American published in the United States, Harriet Wilson's *Our Nig; or, Sketches from the Life of a Free Black* (1859).

After being abandoned by her mother at the age of six, Frado begins a period of indenture in the New England home of the Bellmonts. She quickly becomes a favorite of men working around the farm, who "were always glad to hear her prattle" (37). However, Frado is soon silenced. When young Mary Bellmont accuses Frado of pushing her into a stream, Frado's true account of events is ignored. Mrs. Bellmont, with the aid of her daughter, beats Frado, props her mouth open with a piece of wood, and locks her in a dark room. Frado cannot even talk things over with herself, as many of us are wont to do in times of extreme distress.

As Frado grows older, the Bellmonts' son James, Aunt Abby, and Mr. Bellmont himself all try to shield her somewhat from Mrs. Bellmont's cruelty. But her mistress only becomes more selective and clandestine about the beatings, never failing to warn Frado that she wouldn't hesitate to "cut her tongue out" if she exposed her (72), threatening to do physically to Frado what she has been accomplishing symbolically all along. Frado tells anyway as her voice, encouraged by her advocates, is gaining in strength, which prompts a desperate Mrs. Bellmont to resort to one of her favorite techniques. She forces a wooden block into Frado's mouth and whips her with a rawhide strap.

Frado is undeterred. She reads and continues to converse with those willing to entertain her. And in the novel's climactic scene, when Mrs. Bellmont raises a stick to strike Frado because she feels Frado is taking too long with her chores, Frado loudly declares that if she is struck, she will never work again. Mrs. Bellmont, amazed at the direct verbal challenge, declines to test Frado's resolve. Frado, her period of indenture nearing its conclusion, becomes intensely interested in a wide range of reading material and pursues literacy with vigor. She keeps a book nearby even as she toils.

Charles W. Chesnutt explores nineteenth-century expression/repression conflict against a Southern backdrop, particularly in his Uncle Julius tales. He illustrates how tightly the voices and literate behaviors of slaves were monitored by slave owners. Dave, the central character in "Dave's Neckliss," hardworking and obedient, encounters no special problem with his master until he is found reading the Bible. Dave uses his wit, however, to escape trouble. Mars Dugal, in contrast, cunningly attempts to reinforce control. As Julius narrates:

> "'Dis yer is a se'ious matter,' sezee; 'it's 'g'in de law ter l'arn niggers how ter read, er 'low 'em ter hab books. But w'at yer l'arn out'n dat Bible, Dave?"
>
> "Dave w'an't no fool, ef he wuz a nigger, en sezee: "Marster, I l'arns dat it's a sin fer ter steal, er ter lie, er fer ter want w'at doan b'long ter yer; en I l'arns fer ter love de Lawd en ter 'bey my marster.'
>
> "Mars Dugal' sorter smile' en laf' ter hisse'f, like he 'uz might'ly tickle' 'bout sump'n, en sezee: "'Doan 'pear ter me lack readin' de Bible done yer much harm, Dave. Dat's w'at I wants all my niggers fer ter know. Yer keep right on readin', en tell de yuther han's w'at yer be'n tellin' me. How would yer lack fer ter preach ter de niggers on Sunday?'" (134)

When Dave later is framed for a theft, his Bible is taken away and burned by the overseer.

African American writers have never lost sight of the language problematics posed by Wilson and Chesnutt. Toni Morrison, for one, always foregrounds, perhaps most notably in *Beloved*, the dialectic of expression/repression. Sixo, one of the Garner slaves, a bit more fiery than Dave, decides to stop speaking English because he sees no future in doing so. One can sympathize with Sixo's position after witnessing the conversation, a thoroughly postmodern

one, between him and schoolteacher when Sixo is accused of stealing a pig:

> "You stole that shoat didn't you?"
>
> "No, sir. I didn't steal it."
>
> Schoolteacher smiled. "Did you kill it?"
>
> "Yes, sir. I killed it."
>
> "Did you butcher it?"
>
> "Yes, sir."
>
> "Did you cook it?"
>
> "Yes, sir."
>
> "Well, then. Did you eat it?"
>
> "Yes, sir. I sure did."
>
> "And you telling me that's not stealing?"
>
> "No, sir. It ain't."
>
> "What is it then?"
>
> "Improving your property, sir."
>
> "What?"
>
> "Sixo plant rye to give the high piece a better chance. Sixo
> take and feed the soil, give you more crop. Sixo take and feed Sixo
> give you more work." (190)

Schoolteacher beats Sixo anyway to show him that, as the authorial voice puts it, "definitions belonged to the definers—not the
defined" (190). Of course, Sixo knows this by then, and he seeks to
become a definer. So he leaves the masters their language, only re-
sorting to English again while formulating plans to escape. His
plan is defeated, but he goes to his death singing his own song,
laughing, and calling out, because his Thirty-Mile Woman (not
her master's label) is pregnant, "Seven-O! Seven-O!" (226).

Baby Suggs also practices self-definition. After her freedom is
purchased by her son and she is escorted out of bondage by Mr.
Garner, she asks why she was always referred to as Jenny. Garner
informs her, naturally, that the name on her invoice is Jenny Whi-
tlow. She bitterly rejects it. Another of the story's free elders has
cast aside his given name of Joshua and renamed himself Stamp
Paid because he feels he has settled any debt he might have owed in
this world.

If Zora Neale Hurston and Ralph Ellison have written the
most artistic "discovery of voice" books in the African American
literary tradition, then *Beloved* will probably go down as the most
accomplished "claim your name" book. It is *The Bluest Eye*, though,
that conveys most powerfully Morrison's concern with both the
debilitating and therapeutic aspects of overall language practices.

The story opens with a paragraph that could have been excerpted from a typical primer: "Here is the house. It is green and white. It has a red door. It is very pretty. Here is the family. Mother, Father, Dick, and Jane live in the green-and-white house. They are very happy" (7).

The major trouble with primers is that characteristically they have depicted the happy, white, suburban, nuclear family, which discounts the reality of most of the nation including, of course, African American children like Pecola Breedlove, who wishes for, above all things, a set of blue eyes.

In the second paragraph of the novel, Morrison repeats the wording of the first, only she removes standard punctuation marks. The spaces between the lines of type are smaller. In the third paragraph, she removes the spaces between the words and even ignores conventional syllabification.

The reader soon realizes, even more so as similar phrases are repeated at the outset of later chapters, that a narrative of domination contributes directly to Pecola's plight and eventual insanity. Undeniably, there are other crucial factors: neglect, abuse, incest, rape. But the fact that no voice is stronger to Pecola than the one that encourages self-loathing is an essential element. So is the fact that her father, Cholly Breedlove, who eventually passes the sickness of his life to her, hasn't grabbed hold of an enabling tale. In describing Cholly's relationship with his wife, Morrison pens a line reminiscent of the description of *Native Son*'s Bigger Thomas: "He poured out on her the sum of all his *inarticulate fury and aborted desires*" (emphasis mine) (37).

Contradistinct to the inadequate language system most available to Pecola are the rich verbal experiences shared by Claudia and Frieda MacTeer, who habitually tune in to the vibrant verbal interplay of their mother and her friends. As Claudia narrates:

> Their conversation is like a gently wicked dance: sound meets sound, curtsies, shimmies, and retires. Another sound enters but is upstaged by still another: the two circle each other and stop. Sometimes their words move in lofty spirals; other times they take strident leaps, and all of it is punctuated with warm-pulsed laughter— like the throb of a heart made of jelly. The edge, the curl, the thrust of their emotions is always clear to Frieda and me. We do not, cannot, know the meaning of all her words, for we are nine and ten years old. So we watch their faces, their hands, their feet, and listen for truth in timbre. (16)

With ready access to a collaborative, self-affirming language community, the MacTeer girls have a shield against the dominant narrative.

Morrison's work advances significantly the African American literary project. Although not all characters in the tradition successfully counteract repression, many do achieve autonomy, expressive and otherwise. African American literature as a whole, much like protective African American rumor mechanisms, has been a grand gesture toward healing.

Rap, at its best, is on the same mission. A blend of urgent beats and reinvigorating Black orality, rap is recent testimony that the contesting Black voice in every generation will somehow force itself upon a broad audience. Ready or not, brand new flava will be kicked in your ear. Referring to the Stop the Violence Movement and HEAL (Human Education Against Lies), and to stars like KRS-One and Chuck D, Houston Baker argues that "these positive sites of rap are as energetically productive as those manned by our most celebrated black critics and award winning writers" (59–60). Baker, one of those celebrated critics, sees the connection between "this DJ be Warren G" and "this PHD be Houston B." He adds that "rap is the form of audition in our present era that utterly refuses to sing anthems of, say, STATE homogeneity." (96–97).

Tricia Rose, one of the most informed people on the planet about rap, amplifies Baker's comments:

> Rap music is, in many ways, a hidden transcript. Among other things, it uses cloaked speech and disguised cultural codes to comment on and challenge aspects of current power inequalities. Not all rap transcripts directly critique all forms of domination; nonetheless, a large and significant element in rap's discursive territory is engaged in symbolic and ideological warfare with institutions and groups that symbolically, ideologically, and materially oppress African Americans. (100–101)

Obscenity trials, widespread media attention, and the multibillion scramble over rap revenues indicate the power and importance of this verbal form. Also interesting is the elbowing over who gets to tell the most persuasive academic story about rap. The participation of Skip Gates in the 2 Live Crew trial is called careerism by Baker, who sees Gates as an uninformed outsider pimping the music for publicity. Baker, in turn, is criticized by Rose for marginalizing the female voice in his version of rap's origin and development. And Tricia, just beware. I don't know who is right on these questions, but it's amusing and gratifying to see rap on the agendas of professors at Harvard, Penn, and NYU.

General African American literacy initiatives have run parallel to folkloric and artistic concerns with language power. Immediately after the Civil War, Black folk took the lead on the issue of literacy and schooling for the newly freed population. Black illiteracy had been state-sanctioned, so it is little wonder that a widespread Black literacy project was conceived primarily as a self-help endeavor. These educational pioneers understood that to be literate was to be able to construct textual knowledge for oneself. They didn't want former slaves to be tricked by the textual interpretations of others, as was often the case during slavery when a literate ruling class would lie to slaves about the contents of abolitionist writing. It is common nowadays to hear the slogan "knowledge is power" associated with African American educational campaigns, but Thomas Holt reveals that the phrase has been in use at least since 1865, when the South Carolina Black Men's Convention used it in the preamble to a resolution to establish schools.

Holt also demonstrates quite clearly that there has been no greater dedication to the ideal of popular education in this nation's history than that made by the African American community in the South. The secret schools that operated during slavery, the free schools that were founded shortly after the war, contributions of money that were an amazingly high percentage of contributors' incomes, abundant in-kind resources made available, even the institution of voluntary tax collection systems to support schools when federal and state monies were withheld all constitute remarkable commitment.

The African American literacy project even survived, though barely, both the postreconstruction white backlash and the subsequent attempts of philanthropists like Rosenwald and Rockefeller to gain control of the agenda and ensure that Blacks received only the type of education that kept them "in place," so to speak, in Southern society—a sort of Booker T. Washington deal. W. E. B. Du Bois, as one probably would suppose, was prominent among the African American leadership who countered this idea. But, as Holt writes, opposition came also, and perhaps more importantly in terms of history, from another formidable source:

> Resistance also came from students at Tuskeegee, Fisk, Howard, and Hampton who, during the 1920s, went on strike against their school administrations and in many cases succeeded in getting new

leadership. In the long run, all those struggles laid the basis for the student warriors during the civil rights movement in the late 1950s and early 1960s, because, next to the church, southern colleges were the most critical to the success of that movement. (p. 99)

One thing that now has to happen is that we tap into the fundamental valuation of education that exists to this day in the African American community. Although African Americans have become highly skeptical about certain educational practices and remain dismayed because even institutional certification ensures equal opportunity for them only sporadically, they still view effective schooling to be a key aspect of communal healing. It still represents great possibility.

Language professionals can help to improve educational practice by bringing clarity to discussions of language-related matters. They can share state-of-the-art knowledge about language acquisition and verbal processing and assess how instructional designs are consonant or inconsistent with this information. In addition, they can indicate some of the social variables that affect language instruction and stress, above all, the importance of honoring the language varieties that students bring to school. The teacherly impulse to eradicate specific dialects, for example, is wrong, as Peter Trudgill cogently argues, on grounds of psychology, sociology, and practicality (80–81). Such corrective attempts usually send the message that students are inherently deficient and fail to facilitate expansion of students' verbal repertoires. Students may, in turn, understanding the message clearly, make language a site of resistance and thus reject Standard English so as to solidify their rebellious identities. Some think that these concerns, particularly as they relate to African American students, were laid to rest back in the 1970s. However, that is not the case.

On November 28, 1992, the *New York Times* ran a front-page story entitled "Caribbean Pupils' English Seems Barrier, Not Bridge." The article dealt with the poor performance of students from the English-speaking Caribbean, who were enrolling by the thousands in New York City public schools. To some extent, dialect was cited as the cause of failure, and I was reminded of the Black English debates of previous decades (which continue today, though more quietly). Wary about the impact this article could have, I was eager to author a response and shake things up a bit.

Fortuitously, a reporter from the *Carib News* visited me to solicit my opinion. I told him that if folks are committed to discrimination, they can almost always use language as a pretext. I further expressed that the problem was one of method, not language. It has been demonstrated repeatedly, especially during the celebrated King case (or Black English trial) in 1979, that inappropriate *responses* to language diversity, not language diversity per se, are a major educational problem. I definitely favored committing as much support as possible to helping the students in question; linking dialect with deficiency is what I was mainly arguing against.

I am fully aware of, and do not want to minimize, differences among Black English and a variety of Caribbean dialects. On the other hand, I feel a diasporic view with regard to African-derived language forms yields the most compelling analysis. Only diaspora aesthetics can properly explain rap, for instance, which could not have started as it did without Kool DJ Herc and other Jamaicans. And both Black English and Black Caribbean dialects are examples of what linguist John Holm terms *Atlantic Creoles*. The *Times* article, in fact, describing the language patterns of Caribbean students, reported that "Many forgo the past tense, drop the verb to be (he tall; she a princess) and switch subject and object pronouns (I tell she; him say). They express plurals and possessives differently (two house, or de house-dem; this is mines). Their words often carry different meanings, pronunciation varies greatly and sentence stresses fall in different places" (p. 22). Every item mentioned here, with the possible exception of "de house-dem," is familiar to anyone who knows Black English.

Unfortunately, the reporter lumped my response with those of several other interviewees, not all of whom shared my views or academic background, in a piece entitled "American English Experts Respond!" As a group, we sounded as if there were no real problem at all. I wasn't surprised, then, when "Caribbean English Specialists Respond" appeared in a subsequent issue of the paper. A Caribbean scholar took us to task for being unqualified to address the matter; buying into West-Indians-as-cream-of-the-crop mythology; failing to properly understand the realities of bilingualism and bidialectalism; and ignoring the fact that the children were doing abysmally in school, scoring very low on standardized tests, and sitting in special education classes in disproportionate numbers.

I responded with a letter to the editor, which was graciously printed. I highlighted again that I objected to any belief that dialect differences alone can account for the rate of so-called failure in our schools. I conceded the fact of bilingualism, as there is the issue of mutual unintelligibility between English and certain varieties of Caribbean creoles. But I warned that we must not conflate bilingualism with bidialectalism.

I remain supportive of serious attempts to enhance academic performances of Caribbean students both in class and on standardized tests. Programs that recognize the uniqueness of the Caribbean immigrant experience and build upon strengths in that experience make sense to me. But a reassessment of standardized tests is also required, as is the deconstruction of special education. It's easy to wind up there if you're Black, no matter which sounds come out of your mouth.

I don't pretend that my analysis has drastically effected change. It's merely illustrative of the insight that language professionals can offer. To fully implement correct, not simply corrective, language pedagogy, a varied action agenda is needed along with participation from many types of individuals and groups. Schools ultimately are sensitive to occurrences in the larger society. Anyone working toward positive social change is to some extent helping to strengthen language instruction.

One more flashback as we move forward. Arna Bontemps explains that during the eighteenth century, when even greater than usual pressure was being applied to repress the literacy of slaves, the beautiful, gorgeously double-voiced spirituals were born. As noted earlier, the contesting Black voice will find a way. Marveling at that achievement, James Weldon Johnson paid homage to those artists in "O Black and Unknown Bards," some of which goes:

> There is a wide, wide wonder in it all,
> That from degraded rest and servile toil
> The fiery spirit of the seer should call
> These simple children of the sun and soil.

It's a beautiful poem, but it's also a script we want to flip. We want to bring all the righteousness of African American expressive and intellectual output to bear full force upon the creation of more Black *known* bards whose production will be wide and wonderful as well.

Works Cited

Baker, Houston A. *Black Studies, Rap, and the Academy.* Chicago: The U of Chicago P, 1993.

Chesnutt, Charles W. "Dave's Neckliss" (1889). In Sylvia L. Render, ed., *The Short Fiction of Charles Chesnutt.* Washington, D.C.: Howard UP, 1981. 132–41.

Gilyard, Keith. "Disappointed with Dr. Irish." *Carib News,* June 9, 1993, p. 19.

Gutman, Herbert G. "Schools for Freedom: The Post-Emancipation Origins of Afro-American Education." In Ira Berlin, ed., *Power and Culture: Essays on the American Working Class.* New York: Pantheon, 1987. 260–97.

Holm, John A. *Pidgins and Creoles: Reference Survey.* Cambridge: Cambridge UP, 1989.

————. *Pidgins and Creoles: Theory and Structure.* Cambridge: Cambridge UP, 1988.

Holt, Thomas. "'Knowledge is Power': The Black Struggle for Literacy." In Andrea A. Lunsford, Helene Moglen, and James Slevin, eds., *The Right to Literacy.* New York: Modern Language Association, 1990. 91–102.

Ien, Seymour. "American English Experts Respond!" *Carib News,* Feb. 2, 1993, p. 6.

Irish, George. "Caribbean English Specialists Respond." *Carib News,* Feb. 16, 1993, p. 38.

Johnson, James Weldon. "O Black and Unknown Bards." In James Weldon Johnson, ed., *The Book of American Negro Poetry* (1931). New York: Harcourt Brace: 1969. 123–24.

Morrison, Toni. *Beloved.* New York: Knopf, 1987.

————. *The Bluest Eye* (1970). New York: Washington Square Press, 1972.

Rose, Tricia. *Black Noise: Rap Music and Black Culture in Contemporary America.* Hanover, NH: Wesleyan UP, 1994.

Sontag, Deborah. "Caribbean Pupils' English Seems Barrier, Not Bridge." *New York Times,* Nov. 28, 1992, pp. 1, 22.

Trudgill, Peter. *Sociolinguistics: An Introduction.* Harmondsworth: Penguin, 1974.

Turner, Patricia A. *I Heard It through the Grapevine: Rumor in African-American Culture.* Berkeley: U of California P, 1993.

Williams, John A. *The Man Who Cried I Am* (1967). New York: Thunder's Mouth Press, 1985.

Wilson, Harriet E. *Our Nig; or, Sketches from the Life of a Free Black* (1859). New York: Random House, 1983.

Wright, Richard. *Native Son.* New York: Harper, 1940.

GETTING OFF THE HOOK
—I MEAN CURVE

SHORTLY AFTER THE PUBLICATION of Richard Herrnstein and Charles Murray's tome on intelligence and social policy, I began to have a recurring and disturbing dream. I would be trapped between the covers of the *New York Times Book Review* impaled on a bell curve. I was an African American hanged one of the new ways, that is, by genteel and intellectual klansmen wearing robes of academe. "They just never stop," I would repeat in resignation until I lost consciousness.

In my waking hours I cannot afford to be resigned, precisely because, in fact, they never do cease and desist. Herrnstein and Murray's unleashing of *The Bell Curve: Intelligence and Class Structure in American Life* is a massive and dangerous reinsertion of social Darwinism and biological determinism into public discourse, particularly debates about how best to address issues of so-called racial inequality.

The advice to government officials from the authors, two Harvard graduates, is grim: you need not do a great deal because social problems are determined by low IQs, which are generally unresponsive to programs of social improvement. Affirmative action, it follows, will not yield much benefit; one can hardly hope to

Presented May 20, 1995, at a conference entitled "Educating People of African Descent for the Twenty-First Century," sponsored by the Medgar Evers College Psychology Club and the New York Association of Black Psychologists.

influence the biological design that accords less intelligence to Blacks than to whites. Attempting to hide behind a shield of scientific neutrality, though in reality their scientifically racist backsides are exposed, Herrnstein and Murray provide powerful, if polluted, ideological fuel for the Gingrich Gang.

Fortunately, many voices, including several from Harvard, have risen in opposition, a chorus I must join. I owe it to ancestors, elders, brethren, and progeny. I take no solace in, and as no compliment, the fact that Herrnstein and Murray would have found me remarkable, an African American who scored well on IQ tests. Herrnstein, recently deceased, who made his first public splash as an apologist for Arthur Jensen in the early 1970s, helped to oppress my ethnic group. As does Murray.* This is why I am in on the action.

The Bell Curve was released just as I was about to submerge myself in some good old Afro-rhetoric by reading the first volume of *Speech and Power*, a collection of African American essays edited by Gerald Early. I had meant to appropriate some rhetorical moves in general. The mission quickly changed to a frenzied one of *inventio*, the discovery of specific arguments to counter those of Herrnstein and Murray. Not surprisingly, W. E. B. Du Bois, a Harvard man as well, provides the first.

In a 1920 essay entitled "On Being Black," Du Bois sarcastically notes a range of discriminatory practices by whites, then ponders the intriguing, as he calls them, Souls of White Folk. Anticipating Herrnstein and Murray, or already aware of early-twentieth-century Herrnstein-Murray antecedents (they never do stop), Du Bois writes: "And yet as they preach and strut and shout and threaten, crouching as they clutch at rags of facts and fancies to hide their nakedness, they go twisting, flying by my tired eyes and I see them ever stripped—ugly, human" (6).

No doubt, Du Bois would have much to say about the facts and fancies in *The Bell Curve*. But even seventy-five years ago, in a comment following the one cited above, he indicates perhaps the

---

*Psychologist Arthur Jensen has argued that there are differences of IQ between whites and Blacks that are attributable to genetics and largely immutable. In 1971, Herrnstein echoed this sentiment in an essay entitled "I.Q." that appeared in *Atlantic Monthly*, and he expanded his claims in a 1973 book, *IQ in the Meritocracy*. Twenty-four articles written or coauthored by Jensen are included in the bibliography of *The Bell Curve*. Before now, Murray was best known for his conservative 1984 treatise, *Losing Ground: American Social Policy, 1950–1980*.

best line of argument against works in which much of the analysis revolves around so-called racial differences as he, in essence, rejects the notion of races. Du Bois remarks:

> The discovery of personal whiteness among the world's peoples is a very modern thing—a nineteenth and twentieth century matter, indeed. The ancient world would have laughed at such a distinction. The Middle Ages regarded skin color with mild curiosity; and even up into the eighteenth century we were hammering our national manikins into one, great, Universal Man, with fine frenzy which ignored color and race even more than birth. Today we have changed all that, and the world in a sudden, emotional conversion has discovered that it is white and by that token, wonderful! (6)

Du Bois understands *whiteness* as a linguistic tag that validates the experience and privilege of the *one* at the expense of the *other*. It is a label of political dominance. To be sure, he has not in his essay thought through the deconstruction of whiteness thoroughly. Not able to escape totally the prevailing racialized constructs of his time (nor have enough current scholars escaped the dominant thinking of his time), Du Bois occasionally refers to race as an objective category. Nonetheless, his commentary points to contemporary considerations about race that bear directly upon the worth of *The Bell Curve* as science. Inasmuch as some of the book's central arguments rely heavily on a distinction between a white race and a black one, the arguments necessarily suffer to the same degree that such distinction is shown to be invalid. Yank the pillar of race from beneath Herrnstein and Murrray's logical edifice, and the edifice begins to crumble.

Some of the pull comes from Steven Holmes who, in "Defining Race," asserts that "racial categories, especially in the United States, are often more poetry than science. American blacks almost invariably have some white ancestry, so their classification has more to do with politics and culture than with genes" (273).

Holmes reports that in a 1985 survey of anthropologists, only half the respondents agreed that race is a legitimate biological category. I am slightly amazed that the percentage was still so high, given that no one has ever adequately defined how human beings, Homo sapiens, break down into races. The most commonly talked about physical characteristic, skin color, is only one trait among thousands, hardly enough, at least one wouldn't think, to sustain a theory of races. I am not aware that anyone strictly bases racial groupings on human blood types, though it seems to me that blood type is at least as important as skin color, as anyone who has needed a transfusion should attest. Even if one tries to use skin color to conform to some American classification ideal of black and white, what does one label the East Indians or Arabs, many of whom are darker than I?

Blackness and *whiteness* as human labels are social constructions and signify specific conveniences. When Billy Paul sang "Am I Black enough for you?" he was talking not about genes but ideas. *Whiteness*, as Du Bois well knew, is a term that lends rhetorical sanction to societal inequity. And when white folk call us *blacks*, they are generally not calling us anything more complex or flattering than not white, the other. All this semantic juggling or race talk is to be expected in the expressly racialized social arena America is, but it cannot make for good physical science or even good conversation about physical science.

Herrnstein and Murray are acutely aware of the problem and try hard to tiptoe their way around it. As they explain:

> We frequently use the word *ethnic* rather than *race*, because race is such a difficult concept to employ in the American context. What does it mean to be black in America, in racial terms, when the word black (or African-American) can be used for people whose ancestry is more European than African? How are we to classify a person whose parents hail from Panama but whose ancestry is predominantly African? Is he a Latino? A black? The rule we follow here is to classify people according to the way they classify themselves. The studies of "blacks" or "Latinos" or "Asians" who live in America generally denote people who say they are black, Latino, or Asian— no more, no less. (271)

Cognizant of the impossibility of making real and physically scientific divisions concerning race, the authors resort to a curiously unscientific procedure. They accept what people say. We don't accept the simple declarations of motorists that they are sober when, in fact, they are drunk, yet Herrnstein and Murray would have us trust self-report on an issue that, by their own admission, is quite complicated. They try to turn a laudatory cultural stance, the acceptance of self-naming, into plausible biology. And it just isn't. Nor is their rhetoric of acceptance genuine, for on the very same page they write that "opting for common usage and simplicity, we usually use *black* instead of *African American* and *white* (which always refers to non-Latino whites) instead of *European-American* or *Anglo*" (271).

So what is all their fuss about? Despite protestations to the contrary, Herrnstein and Murray insist on keeping much of their discourse locked in black and white, as it were. Common use and simplicity mean more to them than good science. They care nothing at all about the cultures of African Americans, Latinos, or Asians. They care about objective categories of race, which are actually more of a concern for talk-show producers or hosts, Oprah, Ricki, Geraldo, and the like, than for serious scientists.

Manning Marable, in his almost mandatory "On Being Black" essay, published sixty-one years after the one by Du Bois, contributes a materialist slant to an understanding of *The Bell Curve*, a quality absent from most of the public debate about the book. To Marable, racism is a systemic feature of Western capitalism and functions to "withdraw the dominant group's sympathy from an 'inferior' race, to facilitate its exploitation" (23). Along with such factors as the disproportionate appropriation of African American labor and widespread segregation, racist societies like the United States are also characterized by ideologies that justify these practices. As Marable explains: "Whites as a group have historically approached blacks not in the light of their 'blackness'—perhaps a better term would be 'Africanness'—but in light of what whites believed that blacks must become from the vantage point of their own 'whiteness.' Racist societies must invent 'the Negro.'" (26).

The Negro, or black, is a mechanism that Herrnstein and Murray, who provide intellectual blessing to the existing social order, cannot bring themselves to discard, precisely because they are confirmed, privileged, and content—not to mention white—members of that order. For all their talk about deterministic encounters of the biological kind, they fail to account sufficiently for the social forces driving their own work, and it's no coincidence that the social outlook they articulate at the end of their book supports further segregation and economic disparity. They dismiss the idea that government intervention is a useful way to address social inequality; they're still pushing "trickle-down" economic theory; they entertain visions of a "high-tech and more lavish version of the Indian reservation for some substantial minority of the nation's population" (526). In insisting that the prevailing reality of the twenty-first century will be the reality of the cognitive line, a proposition neither Du Bois nor Marable would accept, and then factoring so-called race into how that line will be drawn (sorry, most folks of color, but you happen to be on the wrong side of it), the authors of

The Bell Curve predictably, so predictably, serve as academic representatives of American racism.

I will not, however, make too strong a case for institutional determinism, as there are members of the academy— of Harvard, in fact—who are highly critical, based upon their own readings of their disciplines, of the type of thinking represented in *The Bell Curve*. Howard Gardner, for example, argues in his celebrated volume, *Frames of Mind: The Theory of Multiple Intelligences*, that IQ is a simplistic and counterproductive way of assessing intellectual capacities:

> If we are to encompass adequately the realm of human cognition, it is necessary to include a far wider and more universal set of competencies than has ordinarily been considered. And it is necessary to remain open to the possibility that many—if not most—of these competences do not lend themselves to measurement by standard verbal methods, which rely heavily on a blend of logical and linguistic abilities. (X)

In addition to linguistic and logical-mathematical capacities, Gardner considers musical, spatial, and bodily kinesthetic intelligences, as well as a set of abilities he terms *personal intelligences*. In his view, not only is intelligence irreducible to a single number on an IQ test, it is not even restricted to the range of abilities measured by such a test. Furthermore, Gardner believes a cultural approach to understanding intelligences yields richer explanations than purely genetic approaches, arguing, after noting the high heritability of physical and temperamental traits, that "when one comes to aspects of cognitive style or personality, the case for high heritability is far less convincing" (35).

Herrnstein and Murray reject Gardner's theory on grounds of both terminology and methodology. They insist that proficiency in, say, music represents talent, not intelligence. Gardner, for his part, would accept this designation, but only on the condition that skill in linguistic and logical-mathematical operations be conversely regarded as talent, not intelligence. Obviously, this subdebate won't be resolved anytime soon, nor will the one about methodology, as Herrnstein and Murray suggest that Gardner's work, which is narrative, is an inappropriate approach to issues they construe to be quantitative. They steadfastly maintain that the weight of statistical evidence supports the claim that intelligence is a general ability, signified by what is known in psychology as the g factor, and that IQ tests measure it accurately.

Gardner, however, does not go quietly. In a review of *The Bell Curve*, he writes:

> Science goes far beyond the number-crunching stereotype; scientific inquiry involves the conceptualization of problems, decisions about the kinds of data to secure and analyze, the consideration of alternative explanations, and, above all, the chain of reasoning from assumptions to findings to inferences. In this sense, the science in *The Bell Curve* is more like special pleading, based on a biased reading of the data, than a carefully balanced assessment of current knowledge. (62–63)

Then shifting gears, reminding us bluntly of the so-called racial ideas entwined with psychometric considerations in *The Bell Curve*, Gardner, after mentioning his debate with Murray on National Public Radio, states:

> Herrnstein and Murray, of course, have a right to their conclusions. But if they truly believe that blacks will not be hurt by the hints that they are genetically inferior, they are even more benighted—dare I say, even more stupid—than I have suggested. (72)

Stephen Jay Gould, commenting on *The Bell Curve* in a piece entitled "Mismeasure by Any Measure," contends that the authors fail to employ sophisticated enough mathematical procedures and that, in reality, they don't make much of a case either for the existence of g or the worth of an IQ score. Gould adds that a proper understanding of statistical procedures reveals that "their own data indicate that IQ is not a major factor in determining variation in nearly all the social behaviors they study—and so their conclusions collapse, or at least become so greatly attenuated that their pessimism and conservative social agenda gain no significant support" (11).

By debunking race theory, seriously challenging restrictive concepts of intelligence, and casting considerable doubt on procedure, one significantly dispels the logical power of *The Bell Curve*. Even so, the book has plenty of spunk left. It's a slick text, relying heavily upon equivocation as a defense strategy. Also, on offense, its authors extend their rhetorical left hand for a shake while trying to clobber you with their right. For example, they agree that intelligence is ranked too highly among human virtues but spend more than eight hundred pages ranking it as highly as they can.

At the outset of the section entitled "Cognitive Classes and Social Behavior," they admit that "you cannot predict what a given person will do from his IQ score," but then they declare immediately that "large differences in social behavior separate groups of people when the groups differ intellectually on average" and further maintain that "intelligence itself, not just its correlation with socioeconomic status, is responsible for these group differences" (117). While admitting the silliness of trying to establish causality between IQ and behaviors such as crime and welfare dependency at the level of individuals, they offer some group correlations and then argue, without properly factoring in social explanations, that lower IQ causes such behaviors. They feature statistics but omit adequate explanations of what the statistics may mean.

Were I to commit crimes, Herrnstein and Murray obviously would not submit that the acts are driven by IQ or, by extension, genes. Were I to organize, by tapping into senses of rage, frustration, and powerlessness caused by life in the racist, economically exploitative U.S.A., a large crew of "blacks" to commit crimes along with me, then in Herrnstein and Murray's view, our actions become explainable by IQ and genetics.

What IQ predicts at best, and I think this point is fairly noncontroversial, is educability or performance within given participant structures, usually those, like school, that emphasize linguistic operations and linear logic within certain cultural contexts and contain embedded in those contexts messages about power and the relative worth of cultures. I would expect groups that don't fare well in, say, school, whose members have often decoded, even if subconsciously, negative "power" signals as inscribed in society at large, often long before they take intelligence exams, to have lower IQs. The scores, more than anything else, reflect that school as generally structured is not designed for them to do as well as they can. They, in fact, would be the group most susceptible to "failing." Similarly, once the disappointments and social penalties for not succeeding in school are factored in, I would anticipate significant correlations among IQ, crime, poverty, welfare dependency, and so on. This does not mean those correlations are the most important correlations. The correlation between crime and a specific organizing of school, for example, may be more important than the correlation between crime and IQ. Now, I am not arguing that a given school organization actually causes crime, and neither should Herrnstein and Murray argue that crime is caused by given IQs.

The Bell Curve authors are really conceding that they can tell us virtually nothing about complex people, particularly not complex African Americans, which is a severe flaw. Theirs is a thick book with a thin vision. The tone, however, is not overly threatening. They anesthetize African Americans with disclaimers before they hang them up on the curve, but the important thing to remember is that they hang them nonetheless.

Of the policy recommendations in *The Bell Curve*, I am most concerned in this space, as you would suspect, with those that affect public school education. Herrnstein and Murray argue that the most crucial problem in American education is the underfunding of programs for the cognitively gifted, we really should say IQ gifted, who are being denied sufficient oportunities, in the authors' view, to develop their considerable potential. Not that these students need to be made any more intelligent, mind you. Herrnstein and Murray insist that they will in any event fulfill their genetic destiny to attend elite universities, embark upon distinguished careers, and run the country. But they won't necessarily possess, in Herrnstein and Murray's eyes, the ability to maximize their effectiveness as leaders unless they receive educations in wisdom and are instructed in "their responsibilities as citizens of a broader society" (443). Toward this end, Herrnstein and Murray support voucher systems, tuition tax credits, greater choice for parents about which public schools their children attend, and the rechanneling of funds targeted for disadvantaged students, who, after all, don't have much to gain, to programs for the IQ gifted.

The authors of *The Bell Curve* never explain why everyone shouldn't be instructed more with respect to civic responsibility. It is an informed citizenry, not merely an informed elite, that makes democracy work. Instead, they remain content to submit a characteristic barrage of data about test scores and surveys, with no accompanying social insight, that speaks to the "dumbing down" of education in general, a quality they claim harms the cognitively elite more than anyone else. They never speak of political and cultural tensions in relation to schools. They never address the poor funding of school systems attended by most African Americans and other so-called minorities or the fact that most of the students they identify as cognitively gifted, coming as they do from, in the authors' own admission, economically privileged homes, are already the beneficiaries, despite what the authors say about underfunding for the cognitively gifted, of preferential treatment.

Of course, public schools need to be improved. No one has to labor hard to convince African Americans, who have received some of the worst that public education has to offer. It is fairly easy to understand as well that the gifted, however we define them, ought to be educated more broadly. The ethical sense of the whiz kids who would swarm Wall Street—or D. C., for that matter—could certainly stand some attention. However, the policies advocated by Herrnstein and Murray, rather than representing genuine cures for public problems, invite the undermining and ultimate dismissal of educational efforts to help the majority of our children. Too narrowly focused, and enslaved to a notion of the elite versus the "at risk," the authors of *The Bell Curve* write off millions of nonelite students who are, nevertheless, genetically "at promise," to borrow a phrase from Gardner, and in need of vital nurturing for their potential to be realized.

They never do stop. Nor can we. Sweet dreams.

WORKS CITED

Du Bois, W. E. B. "On Being Black" (1920). In Gerald Early, ed., *Speech and Power: The African American Essay and Its Cultural Content, from Polemics to Pulpit*, vol. 1. Hopewell, NJ: Ecco Press, 1992. 3–7.

Early, Gerald, ed. *Speech and Power: The African American Essay and Its Cultural Content, from Polemics to Pulpit*, vol. 1. Hopewell, NJ: Ecco Press, 1992.

Gardner, Howard. *Frames of Mind: The Theory of Multiple Intelligences* (1983). New York: Basic Books, 1985.

Gould, Stephen Jay. "Mismeasure by Any Measure." In Russell Jacoby and Naomi Glauberman, eds., *The Bell Curve Debate: History, Documents, Opinions*. New York: Times Books, 1995. 3–13.

Herrnstein, Richard J. "I.Q." *Atlantic Monthly*. September, 1971. 43–64.

——. *I.Q. in the Meritocracy*. Boston: Atlantic-Little Brown, 1973.

Herrnstein, Richard J., and Charles Murray. *The Bell Curve: Intelligence and Class Structure in American Life*. New York: Free Press, 1994.

Jacoby, Russell, and Naomi Glauberman, eds. *The Bell Curve Debate: History, Documents, Opinions*. New York: Times Books, 1995.

Holmes, Steven A. "Defining Race." In Russell Jacoby and Naomi Glauberman, eds., *The Bell Curve Debate: History, Documents, Opinions*. New York: Times Books, 1995. 273–75.

Marable, Manning. "On Being Black: The Burden of Race and Class" (1981). In Gerald Early, ed., *Speech and Power: The African American Essay and Its Cultural Content, from Polemics to Pulpit*, vol. 1. Hopewell, NJ: Ecco Press, 1992. 20–28.

Murray, Charles. *Losing Ground: American Social Policy, 1950–1980*. New York: Basic Books, 1984.

A
FINAL
WORD

PLAYING WITH
THE PATTERNS

THERE ARE TWO MAIN reasons I have resisted, despite considerable urging, following up on the memoir sections of my book *Voices of the Self*. One, I don't kiss and tell. So I would have to leave a large hole in a narrative about adult life compared to the small one (barely noticed by some) that I left in the tale of my adolescence. I can work with cracks in my story but not craters. Two, I haven't considered my adulthood to be all that remarkable. Interesting, yes, exciting at times, but nothing I would read a whole lot about— the pressure not so intense, the days not so desperate. However, as two colleagues have set the task for me of reflecting upon some of the values and experiences that account for my teacherly orientation, I find that I can pick up a strand of the story line (lifeline) with which I don't mind playing.*

January 1971. Queensborough Community College. Laid out among the hills and valleys of the former Oakland Country Club in relatively privileged Bayside, Queens. From there you could peep across the city line into even more privileged Nassau County, into Jay Gatsby territory, a fact I would soon learn in an English class.

I made a bit of a splash on the African American social scene, primarily because I was a new face, starting as I did in the middle of

*Dick Larson and Tom McCracken prompted me to write this piece. I intended to submit it for a collection they planned to edit. However, when it grew to be a longer manuscript than they requested, I decided to include it here.

the academic year. The first day of the semester I was walking down a corridor in the Humanities Building when I began to hear all this hoopla. A group of sistas were holding cheerleading practice. But there were no short skirts, oxfords, bobby socks, and pompoms. These sistas were decked out African style, bright-colored bubas, matching géles. Bright greens. Browns and yellows. Verdant, summer, and autumnal beauties bouncing around a classroom in the middle of winter. Fine young women preparing to root for the Queensborough entry in the Black Brothers Basketball League, an alternative to traditional varsity leagues that weren't, one way or another, doing justice to the brothas. The league was supposed to have a political platform, though I never quite figured out what it was. What I do know is that the QCC cheerleaders brought the most flava. And I had a lot of good times with some of those sistas. But remember, we won't go *there*.

I had two courses dealing with the study of communication: English Composition I and Voice and Diction. Comp was fine. I had a whole lot to say and didn't have too much trouble saying it. Whatever the assignment was, I bent it to my purposes. That's how I figured you did it. Show teachers enough of their own style, then bend the rest yo' way. Know what I'm sayin? Even if they give you some passé protocols to work with, you cover them, sign them the way Aretha Franklin or Luther Vandross push against commonplace delivery to place their inimitable vocal signatures on ballads. Of course there's always a tension about just how hard to push, but I was managing quite well. I didn't feel oppressed by the institution's language or that I couldn't write my way into academic conversations. I am now aware of the current voice-versus-social construction argument, you know, whether we should teach students that they write the culture or that the culture writes them. When kept so narrow or dichotomous, the debate is frivolous. I knew I was socially constructed, and I knew I had something peculiar to say about it as well. I saw no contradiction, or at least not one I couldn't live with. Besides, there was an overriding question that held my attention: What's any of this got to do with Black liberation? After a mental hibernation of sorts, I was a bear on the prowl for energetic, even radical, ideas.

The political, then, was important to me along with the affective. As a writing instructor, I try to create spaces for negotiation, innovation, and the exploration of political views. Writing had to mean something to me if I were going to write with meaning. And

I now feel that students who are vested in writing the way I was, in the sense of purposefulness, not necessarily particular persuasion, have the best chance to achieve the writing standards set by academic institutions. The interaction of formal essay writing and vernacular discourse generates specific and valuable verbal structures, thus understandings, not producible in any other way. It can strengthen one's entire intellectual package. Therefore, though I know full well and respect the critique that the implementation of language standards may oppress practitioners of nonstandard varieties, I also think it worthwhile to support the goal of students becoming at least "two ways strong," as Eve Fesl, first Koori (Aboriginal Australian) to receive a Ph.D. in Australia, put the matter, with her fists thrust in the air, at the 1990 conference of the International Federation of Teachers of English. She wasn't kickin no lame or tame bidialectalism for the marketplace rap; she was talking about mastering the language of wider communication as a way of tightenin up, as I said, one's whole intellectual thang, for struggle, for leadership, for whatever. My present articulation of these ideas is post grad school, post a lot of years of teaching, and post encounters with minds like Fesl's. Clearly, though, I already possessed some, we might even say the core, of this sensibility that first semester at QCC.

Voice and Diction was crazy. Unlike the writing placement exam, which I breezed through, I failed the speech test. A professor taped me, listened to me soften the initial consonant cluster for words like *these*, *there*, *their* and *those*; noted how I dragged the vowel sound in *rice* and *ice*; then decided that I had a Southern accent. In my nineteen years I hadn't spent thirty days south of Brooklyn. But according to the professor I somehow had acquired this Southern accent. Me and most of the African Americans, mainly Northerners, too, at QCC. Now we knew a Southern accent, what we called "sounding country," when we heard one. That wasn't what we sounded like. Regardless: Remedial Speech. They had me spinning around for a moment, got me to thinking I was substandard. Had me in the mirror overarticulating and sounding stupid like I was in charm school or something. *These* may have begun to sound a little less like *dese*, but I know that *rice* and *ice* stuff didn't change one iota. Working on that just sounded too dumb, and I wasn't even tryin ta git wit it. At the postsemester taping, I glared at the examiner and then spoke pretty much as I had before. He said I passed.

Back then I hadn't heard about Beryl Bailey, Lorenzo Turner, or William Stewart. J. L. Dillard's *Black English* was still a year away. No one told me I was speaking a systematic, rule-governed variation of English. Even if construed as a problem, my "Southern accent" would not have been sensitive to isolated speech drills I saw as primarily pointless. But things worked out I suppose. I handled my business. I couldn't help noticing, however, that several of my African American classmates never finished the course.

Perhaps the most significant thing about my experience in Voice and Diction is that it was simultaneous with my earning a grade of A- in Composition. I would always recall this as I was working through the literature or listening to presentations about Black English and education. To this day, I'm very suspicious when folks try to lay writing problems at the doorstep of dialect. The analysis has to be deeper. Again, purpose, prior experiences, motivation, perceptions of institutional texts and subtexts all have to be factored into the mix. I was committed to Comp, not voice lessons.

About fifteen years after Voice and Diction, I was invited back to QCC to speak at a language symposium. My old instructor happened to be in the audience, and I told the story of how I had been required to take remedial speech, including the fact that he had done the requiring. He denied that such a thing could have occurred. I suggested we could scoot on over to the registrar's office for a little archival research. He declined.

Back in 1971, there was some serious outside schooling to be continued, a vibrant and vital extracurriculum. Someone had the good sense to build the Langston Hughes Library & Community Cultural Center two blocks from my home. It became my office. When my homies couldn't find me at the crib or out on Northern Boulevard, they began to check the library. Then they started checking the library first. "He probably in his new crib wit dem books," they would say.

That Black liberation question was largely guiding my actions. What could I snatch from books to help Black folk? I read history, political science, psychology. You could obtain a healthy dose of each just by reading Frantz Fanon. *Black Skin, White Masks* and *Wretched of the Earth*. But I read poetry most of all. Black arts, baby. And poetry was king of all that. Creative writing as instrumentality. As Amiri Baraka wrote in "Black Art":

> Put it on him, poem. Strip him naked
> to the world! Another bad poem cracking

128

steel knuckles in a jewlady's mouth
Poem scream poison gas on beasts in green berets
Clean out the world for virtue and love,
Let there be no love poems written
until love can exist freely and
cleanly. Let Black People understand
that they are the lovers and the sons
of lovers and warriors and sons
of warriors Are poems & poets &
all the loveliness here in the world

I wasn't really a cultural nationalist deep down inside. Cultural nationalism was more of a church I liked to visit. Made me feel good, but I wasn't looking for it to carry me too far. I knew serious struggle didn't revolve around cracking "jewladies" in the mouth or leaving references to Black daughters out of your verses. I had more Panther-like leanings (their male chauvinism notwithstanding), employing a social critique that incorporated both ethnicity and class. But even at that, I couldn't cut loose my nationalist bards. I consumed the entire library collection of recent Black poetry. Works by the likes of Baraka, Larry Neal, Don L. Lee (Haki Madhubuti), Sonia Sanchez, Johari Amini, and Carolyn Rodgers. Nikki Giovanni actually visited the library to read. Then I would go on a relentless hunt for even more poems. Uptown to Michaux's on 125th Street. Around to the Liberation Book Store on Lenox Avenue. Running down the material coming out of The East in Brooklyn. Checking the record stores for albums by The Last Poets, The Original Last Poets, Gil Scott-Heron, and Wanda Robinson. Far into most nights, often after I had put my schoolwork to bed, I would work on writing my own poems, mostly inferior agitprop stuff, but some good. I might ease into my sister's room and whisper them in the ear of my sleeping niece, Nicole (Nikki of course), who was born the same week I enrolled at QCC.

We started a poetry group that operated out of the library. Myself, Ahmasi (Ronnie Lloyd), Randy Latimer, Eric Rawlins, Lorraine Taylor, and a few others. We put on poetry shows to read our work, and we also organized readings for other poets from the community. The latter events were probably more fun, as people would sometimes dash in off the street, grab the mike, and make up poems, some of them wine-induced, right on the spot. Hip-hoppers would call it free-stylin. And it was cool, not a whole lot different from the stuff most of the neighborhood poets were laboring to write down. You know the trip. Black King, Black Queen, let's stay tight and rule the universe after we dispense with the racist crackers and honkies. Raw and necessary stuff, but, as I said, I was trying to move beyond it. Make some other kinds of artistic mistakes. Which I surely did.

One night in the Village Vanguard, while listening to McCoy Tyner, I scribbled a poem on a napkin and gave it to him. My action was partly arrogance, partly sloe gin fizz, and partly the suggestion of my main QCC running buddy, Maurice Ford. I later knew that if you wanted to give props to someone as bad as Mc-Coy, you had to come much stronger than a hasty napkin poem. So I disciplined myself to write a longer, stronger poem, "The Piano Man Pulled Some Along," though I doubt he's seen it.

I thought I would eventually place a book with Dudley Randall's Broadside Press or Lee's Third World Press. I think a couple of others in our group felt the same way. In the meantime, since everybody with two sheets of paper and a stapler was publishing poetry, Lorraine, Eric, Randy, and I produced our own anthology near the end of 1971, which we called *White Paper, Black Poem*. Didn't sell much, but I felt it was the perfect way to cap the year.

We also had a newspaper going on. The *Transition Press*. Eric was the editor, and the *New York Times* kicked in some loot in addition to sending newspapermen out to the neighborhood on Saturdays to show us the journalistic ropes. We certainly had enough local data to draw upon, as the Corona–East Elmhurst area was a microcosm of the Black urban situation in America. For example, in just a five-block stretch of Northern Boulevard, say from 100th Street to 105th Street, you had winos lining up outside the liquor store at eight in the morning (let's get our drink on), rampant drug activity around the clock (let's escape reality), storefront Christian churches (let's pray), the liberal, integrationist Walter White Manpower Center (let's overcome, or at least sing about it), the Nation of Islam's Mosque 7A (let's separate from the white devils), the headquarters of the largest branch of the Black Panther Party in New York State (let's off the pig), and the writers in the library (let's figure all this out). Expand the frame of reference just a bit and you could see tensions between home owners and the permanent underclass, between petit bourgeois and "illegitimate capitalist," and peep in on the movement of students going to and from various colleges, from public community colleges (like me) to the Ivy League.

Widen the scope some more. In the spring of 1971, the Panthers split into Newton and Cleaver factions. It's sometimes referred to as the East Coast–West Coast split, but in New York you had both Newton and Cleaver loyalists, which ultimately resulted in the assassination of Cleaver devotee Robert Webb in Harlem and the murder of Newton disciple Sam Napier in Corona, the branch office I mentioned above being set ablaze in the process. I remarked to a numbers runner on my block that the white folks got Webb and Napier. He replied that white folks certainly do their share, but they don't do it all. He warned against turning white folks into God.

The Louis Armstrong funeral was held on 103rd Street. Folks wanted to speak out on George Jackson and Angela Davis. The Attica uprising occurred upstate, and we knew brothas in the middle of it. So, as I said, there was plenty to write about to see if we could get everybody's "right on" on right, as Eric (I think it was) would say.

I remember writing an article about Davis, but not what I actually reported or argued. Whatever it was I had penned failed to meet the approval of a sista, who had spent time in California and was willing to school a young reporter, make him wiser. This took me into Marcuse and Conforth, material like that. And a lot of personal tutoring. Now I can't say much more than that. You know my creed.

Around the same time, I cut into Ramón Jiminez and Hubert Hammond. To this day, I think they are two of the most stellar people I've ever met. They were trying to establish an alternative school, simply called The Community School, and were working out of a storefront a block from the library. Ramón had graduated from St. John's University and had plans to attend Harvard Law School. Hubert had been to Bowdoin College up in Maine. They pushed the Marxist tip but avoided, and this is the main point I want to make about them, being dogmatic. Ramón had already read Freire's *Pedagogy of the Oppressed*. Problem posing was a big part of his manner. Both he and Hubert could teach you a great deal with questions. I like to load up political questions the way they did. If it's just about ethnicity, then why did 15 percent of the African American electorate vote for Reagan? If it's just about class, then why do working-class white Democrats cross party lines to keep nonelitist African American Democratic candidates out of office? We talked 1971 versions of this stuff.

Hubert said there was an important role for Black literature, especially if the political consciousness therein was as sophisticated as possible. Needless to say, he wasn't impressed with any of the poets I talked about. And he never criticized my own work directly (still too nationalist for his taste), though I got his point. Study Richard Wright, he advised.

Ramón had more use for my work. Ordinarily the most ethical person I knew, he would take my poems, change all the African American references to Latino ones, and read his versions before audiences. Then he would laugh and tell everyone (still does) that he was my poetry instructor and that I liked to rip off his poems. Little matter. I owed him.

Ramón worked in an educational program in Harlem with Karen Troupe, who was married to the poet Quincy Troupe, who taught at Richmond College. I knew about him from Woodie King's anthology, *BlackSpirits*, and thought he worked the language better than most poets I read. His "Ode to John Coltrane" set a standard for Coltrane poems that has never been matched. Ramón arranged for me to meet him and even drove me to Quincy's home. I went on ultra-cool, you know, like I was invited to the home of notables all the time. Quincy mostly talked about the need to practice, to pursue the craft. He said political work was necessary but warned that you have to be careful about your running partners. You could be getting whipped up by the police while your crew was hiding around the corner. I knew about that one already, wasn't that naive. We talked about poets we liked. He said Amus Mor out of Chicago was bad. Then he asked the critical question: have you read Pablo Neruda? I had never even heard of Neruda, arguably the greatest poet of the twentieth century, much less read him. So that was the key info that night. I had to go on a Neruda mission.

Latin American surrealism exploded inside my head. Neruda's lines were like verbal depth charges. "A river that the feathers of the burning eagles are covering." I didn't see how you beat that imagery. The first book I bought (done by Robert Bly) also contained translations of Vallejo, who was masterful as well. I rapidly collected more titles, *Residence in Earth*, *The Captain's Verses*, *The Heights of Macchu Picchu*, *Twenty Love Poems and a Song of Despair*, *Selected Poems*, *Five Decades*, *Fully Empowered*, *The Captain's Verses*, *Spain*, *Take This Cup from Me*. Politics or personal passion, the brothas got down.

It seemed that because I was a serious student, I became everybody's favorite one. I had to duck people so they wouldn't add more titles to my list before I could catch up. I had to hole up with Nkrumah's *Conscienceism, Neo-Colonialism: Last Stage of Imperialism,* and *Handbook of Revolutionary Warfare.* Aimé Césaire's *Discourse on Colonialism* and *Return to My Native Land.* Oh Césaire:

> My mouth shall be the mouth of misfortunes which
> have no mouth, my voice the freedoms of those free-
> doms which break down in the prison-cell of despair.

The Community School never became fully operational. It housed a couple of service programs for a while, then folded altogether. Ramón was off to Harvard, where I visited him several times. Once while I was there, he was invited to give a speech at an antiwar rally on Boston Commons. The speakers had to climb up onto a high platform, and Ramón asked a friend of ours, Sonny Bargeron, and me to go up with him. That was the style back then. You spoke while your boys stood in back of you looking militant. I actually was more interested in my conversation with Dr. Daniel Ellsberg, he of the Pentagon Papers case, who was scheduled to speak after Ramón. I was like, "Yo Doc, you gon beat this case or what?" But we didn't get too far because Ramón was ready to begin, and I had to climb on up to the platform.

Ramón affirmed the antiwar efforts before launching into an attack on white leftists for copping out on other issues involving people of color. Somebody threw a whiskey bottle, and I told Ramón it was time to jet. I knew we could handle only so many drunken liberals. But he persevered and kept telling the truth, which is his way.

On those trips to Massachusetts, I picked up yet another mentor, Andrew Vachss. A once and future New Yorker, he was at that time living in Somerville and directing a juvenile facility. Andrew was a stone-cold action man. He could theorize with the best of them, but the bottom line for him was commitment, getting things done. Still is, as you can tell from both his law and writing careers. He's my top advice man to this day.

Extracurricular activity, then, especially the mentors I picked up along the way, figured prominently in my thoughts about learning and teaching. So-called multiculturalism was a given, silly to ignore. And I leaned toward an interactionist, critical mode of inquiry. I was miles ahead of all the talk about critical thinking that came into vogue years later. To me, critical thinking comes with the territory. If you read, write, and discuss texts critically, how could you not be experiencing critical thought? If you ran with the people I ran with, there was no other kind of thinking to do. Similarly, "teaching the conflicts" would be no new wrinkle in classes I was involved in either as student or teacher. It's the only way to be true to the game. Some of my teachers back at QCC thought I was too serious-minded; some were amused. I remember one saying she'd like to see me in twenty-five years. Well, twenty-five years later, one percent of the nation is pocketing forty percent of the national wealth and I'm still willing to beef about it.

My school reading list wasn't nearly so provocative as my outside one. However, there was plenty to debate. I didn't have to wait for reader-response theorists to know it's okay to stretch out on a text. I may have stretched too much at times, but I was never timid. After reading "The Rockpile," for example, a short story by James Baldwin that ends sort of up in the air, I wrote a paper contending that the boy (John) dies at the end, or at least gets hurt badly. My instructor countered that we couldn't assume that. But I felt that the symbolism and internal logic of the story compelled such a conclusion, and that I had made the case. We had to agree to disagree and call it a day. Years later, when I was a graduate student at Columbia, I put the question to Baldwin himself after he visited a class I was in. He didn't seem to recall the story, at least not readily. And I don't know why I thought he should. He was past fifty and had written a couple of million words by then. When I refreshed his memory and pushed the question again, he said the story does not suggest that John is to be assaulted. So I went back and read "The Rockpile" closely. Blood and death, or musings about blood and death, on all the opening pages. "Rockpile" suggesting prison. Seemed like some heavy foreshadowing to me. I won't say Baldwin was wrong, but D. H. Lawrence said that critics have the job of saving stories from the people who write them.

At times, my extracurricular sensibility caused me to take even more decisive action in school. I was enrolled in a poetry workshop and had an instructor whose sense of development, not to mention aesthetics, differed drastically from my own. He liked to call all of us beginning poets. To me, that meant, like, someone in the third grade. I thought of myself as a poet. Period. But in his view, we might, if we were good enough, become promising poets in our twenties, and mature poets after that. He would sound pretty reasonable to me today, but back then, because he had no idea of the circles I moved in, where there seemed to be all kinds of outstanding and mature poets in their twenties, including most of the ones I mentioned earlier, he turned me off. When you also consider that he only seemed familiar with European- style work and championed imitations of Euro-style masters—nary a word about a Neruda or a Troupe in that class—you understand why I dropped the course, the only English course I ever withdrew from in college except for one in which James Fenimore Cooper was threatening to bore me to death. I left the poetry class because the instructor didn't bother to find out what I knew about poetry. Only his tastes, experiences, and the canon he paid homage to mattered. That squeezed me out, which has been instructive to recall.

I also thought about dropping Black American History, oddly enough, and probably would have if my homegirl Gerianne Scott and this brotha from Freeport named Phil hadn't been on the scene to absorb some of the tension. If we challenged, and challenge we did, some of the ideas being taught, the conversation always swung around to how disrespectful young Blacks were compared to older Blacks like the professor, and on the way to that point we had to hear that Black people in the ghetto deface and destroy the very places where they live and thus should stop bellyaching about what society won't do for them, something like that. Freeport Phil, sporting a big Afro and always on the case, stayed the most agitated, even got put out of the class a few times under threat of having security guards summoned. He did more intellectual scuffling than prescribed coursework. You can't effectively help those you don't respect, a fact to bear in mind.

I became an English tutor at QCC, worked for Linda Stanley, whom I still run into at CCCC. I tried to help students correct their errors, and I always had some sort of pep talk for them. They thought writing came easy to me or was a gift. I knew it had more to do with reading and work and practice and a sense of high stakes. Years later, when I was a basic writing adjunct at LaGuardia Community College, my first teaching appointment, I received an evaluation from the director of composition in which she noted that, in preparing the class for the departmental writing exam, I was exhorting the class like a coach preparing a team for the Super Bowl. The coaching metaphor has become popular since then and has a positive connotation, but the director was not complimenting me at the time. And I realized that. I was just disappointed that I couldn't make the test sound more important, to a group of largely African American and Latino basic writers, than a mere football extravaganza.

By the time I left QCC, I had completed eighteen courses, six in English. I had mainly sampled, unconcerned with the specific requirements of the A.A. degree. I transferred into a university-wide baccalaureate program and, praise to the extracurriculum, received life experience credits for various writing projects.

Andrew was back in New York. So was Ramón. I agreed to help them with legal work they were doing in the New Jersey prison system. We'd be regularly off to Rahway, Trenton, way down to Leesburg. Andrew had the idea of shooting a video inside Trenton State Penitentiary. Part of it would show me teaching a writing class we would convene for the occasion. After we rolled the tape, and this was still years prior to LaGuardia CC, I was thinking that I could actually do it. I could teach for real.

INDEX

137

Books in the African American Life Series

Coleman Young and Detroit Politics: From Social Activist to Power Broker, by
Wilbur Rich, 1988

Great Black Russian: A Novel on the Life and Times of Alexander Pushkin, by
John Oliver Killens, 1989

Indignant Heart: A Black Worker's Journal, by Charles Denby, 1989
(reprint)

The Spook Who Sat by the Door, by Sam Greenlee, 1989 (reprint)

Roots of African American Drama: An Anthology of Early Plays, 1858–1938,
edited by Leo Hamalian and James V. Hatch, 1990

Walls: Essays, 1985–1990, by Kenneth McClane, 1991

Voices of the Self: A Study of Language Competence, by Keith Gilyard, 1991

*Say Amen, Brother! Old-Time Negro Preaching: A Study in American
Frustration*, by William H. Pipes, 1991 (reprint)

*The Politics of Black Empowerment: The Transformation of Black Activism in
Urban America*, by James Jennings, 1992

*Pan Africanism in the African Diaspora: An Analysis of Modern Afrocentric
Political Movements*, by Ronald Walters, 1993

*Three Plays: The Broken Calabash, Parables for a Season, and the Reign of
Wazobia*, by Tess Akaeke Onwueme, 1993

*Untold Tales, Unsung Heroes: An Oral History of Detroit's African American
Community, 1918–1967*, by Elaine Latzman Moon, Detroit Urban
League, Inc., 1994

*Discarded Legacy: Politics and Poetics in the Life of Frances E.W. Harper,
1825–1911*, by Melba Joyce Boyd, 1994

African American Women Speak Out on Anita Hill–Clarence Thomas, edited
by Geneva Smitherman, 1995

Lost Plays of the Harlem Renaissance, 1920–1940, edited by James V. Hatch
and Leo Hamalian, 1996

*Let's Flip the Script: An African American Discourse on Language, Literature,
and Learning*, by Keith Gilyard, 1996

H